CONTEMPORARY'S

COMMUNICATION SKILLS THAT WORK

A Functional Approach for Life and Work

BOOK TWO

ELIZABETH ROMANEK

Project Editor
Julie Landau

Consultant
Jorie W. Philippi
Performance Plus Learning
Consultants

CONTEMPORARY
BOOKS

CHICAGO

Credits: pp. 1, 63, 83—© Ralph J. Brunke; p. 7—© 1990 M.
C. Escher Heirs/ Cordon Art, Baarn, Holland; p. 11—©
Spencer Grant/ Stock, Boston; p. 19—© Dawson Jones,
Inc./ Stock, Boston; p. 26—© Rhoda Sidney/ Stock,
Boston; p. 27a—© Robert Frerck/ Odyssey Productions; p.
276—© Lawrence Migdale/ Stock, Boston; p. 35—© Jim
Whitmer; p. 41—© Mark Antman/ Stock, Boston; pp. 41,
126—©—Better Business Bureau of Chicago and Northern
Illinois Consumer Resource Book; p. 55—© Robert V.
Eckert, Jr.,/ Stock, Boston; p. 63—© Consumer Plus Pages,
Chicago Consumer Yellow Pages, Donnelly Directory
Publisher; p. 85—© David Aronson/ Stock, Boston; p. 100—
© Ray Ellis/ Photo Researchers; p. 119—© Cary Wolinsky/
Stock, Boston; p. 131—© The Photo Works/ Photo Researchers

Library of Congress Cataloging-in-Publication Data

Communication skills that work.

    Contents : bk. 1. A functional approach for life and
work / Wendy Stein—bk. 2. A functional approach for
life and work / Elizabeth Romanek.

    1. Communication.   I. Stein, Wendy.
P90.S799   1991   302.2   91-11340
ISBN 0-8092-4122-6
ISBN 0-8092-4121-8

Published by Contemporary Books, Inc.
180 North Michigan Avenue, Chicago, Illinois 60601
Manufactured in the United States of America
International Standard Book Number: 0-8092-4121-8

Published simultaneously in Canada by
Fitzhenry & Whiteside
195 Allstate Parkway
Valleywood Business Park
Markham, Ontario L3R 4T8
Canada

Editorial Director Caren Van Slyke	*Editorial Assistant* Erica Pochis
Editorial Craig Bolt Mark Boone Lisa Black Sarah Carrig Holly Graskewitz Ree Kline Betsy Rubin	*Cover Design* Georgene Sainati *Illustrator* Graziano, Krafft & Zale, Inc. *Art & Production* Carolyn Hopp
Editorial Production Manager Norma Fioretti	*Typography* Ellen Yukel
Production Editor Jean Farley Brown	

Cover photograph © Walter Hodges/Westlight

Contents

To the Student

Welcome to *Communication Skills That Work, Book Two.*
This book is designed to help you learn strategies for
communicating more effectively in everyday life and at
work. In each lesson, you will see how a listening,
speaking, or writing skill is used in everyday life. Then
you will learn to apply that skill on the job. Throughout
the book, you will have many chances to practice
communication skills and to relate them to your own life.

Each chapter contains

- an opening story that puts communication skills in
  a real-life context
- instruction on effective communication skills
- activities that help you practice those skills
- *Working Together*, an activity that involves
  working with one or more other students
- *Problem Solver*, an exercise in which you examine
  a typical on-the-job problem and arrive at
  solutions

Some of the activities in this book require you to work
with a partner or in a group. However, you can complete
most of the activities by yourself. Even if you are not in a
class, you might be able to find another person who will
do some of the partner activities with you.

The book contains a number of *Practice* exercises. There
is an answer key in the back of the book. However, there
are no "right" answers for many of the exercises. As you
think about and discuss the exercises, you will probably
come up with several answers. Always think of good
reasons to support your answer.

We hope that you enjoy this book!

Speaking and Listening

Imagine that you are at a job interview. You probably listen carefully to understand the interviewer's questions. You select your answers thoughtfully, including the facts about your work history that will impress the interviewer. You also monitor your language to make sure you sound businesslike.

Now imagine that you are the interviewer. Most likely, you are asking specific questions to find out whether the interviewee is right for the job. As you listen to the answers, you try to get a sense of the person's attitude and abilities.

At work and in everyday life, clear communication is vital. In Lesson 1 of this book, you will learn about the features of clear communication and assess your own communication needs. Lessons 2 and 3 provide you with specific strategies for listening and speaking more effectively. You will learn to concentrate to better understand what another person is saying. You will also learn how using your background knowledge can help you improve your listening skills.

Lesson 4 explores strategies for nonverbal communication. You send messages all the time without speaking. Your body positions, gestures, and facial expressions convey unspoken messages. By becoming more aware of nonverbal communication, you can get a better idea of what people mean by what they say. You'll also become attuned to what *you* are conveying nonverbally.

In Lessons 5 through 11, you will become more aware of what you need to do to communicate more clearly in

During a job interview, clear communication is vital.

different everyday and workplace situations. For instance, imagine that a stranger approaches you on the street and asks for directions to a nearby subway stop. Your directions must be simple and precise. Similarly, when you instruct a coworker, you need to be clear and concise. Other lessons will cover situations such as community and work-related meetings, personal and business phone calls, and performance evaluations.

The Communication Process

Angela Winters, a TV talk show host, is interviewing Crystal Barnett, a famous movie star. The two women are exchanging stories about the publicity they receive in the tabloid newspapers.*

Angela: Here's a gripe I know we have in common: the tabloid newspapers in the supermarket checkout line.

Crystal: You're right. Those papers love to get your picture on the front page. They twist your words around. They exaggerate or just plain lie about your private life.

Angela: I'll say. According to the tabloids, I have a seventeen-year-old niece who committed armed robbery. I'm an only child, so how could I have a niece?

Crystal: I know what you mean. Some of those trashy stories say that I'm battling alcoholism, starving myself to death, and ruining people's marriages. What really gets me is when they write stories about my kids. I can ignore the garbage about me, but my kids' feelings get hurt. For example, one paper said my teenage daughter is pregnant. Some reporter dug up an old photograph of her, and the paper printed it on the front page.

Angela: That's too bad. Those papers are in the business of spreading rumors and making money. To be honest with you, though, before I became famous, I'd sometimes buy those papers just to amuse myself.

Crystal: So did I! (*laughs*) Some of those headlines really knocked me out: "Elvis Presley Alive! Hiding on a Wyoming Ranch"; "60-year-old Grandmother Gives Birth to Triplets"; "Marilyn Monroe Speaks from Beyond Grave."

Angela: I always liked the headlines about miraculous births. By the way, Crystal, we've got to stop now for a commercial break. Afterward, I want to hear all about your latest movie.

---

*tabloid newspapers—newspapers that publish sensational stories

Talk About It

- Do Angela and Crystal understand each other?
- How can you tell?
- What skills do you need in order to communicate clearly?

What Is Communication?

Communication is a process by which people exchange information. It is a two-way process because it involves both the sending and the receiving of a message. What are the two most common ways you send a message? By speaking and writing. How do you receive a message? By listening and reading. The model at the right illustrates the communication process.

Sending and receiving messages may seem like a simple process. Why, then, are there so many mix-ups and misunderstandings? Communication can be complex and difficult. You can improve your skills by becoming more aware of the situations in which you need to communicate well.

When do *you* need to speak, listen, read, or write carefully? Do you frequently make phone calls? Do you listen to your friends' problems? Do you write letters to friends or relatives? You can learn about your communication needs by observing yourself.

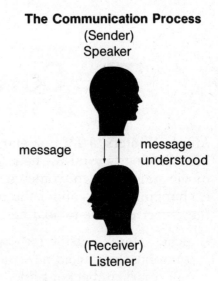

The Communication Process
(Sender)
Speaker

message   message understood

(Receiver)
Listener

Both speaker and listener must actively participate in the communication process. Each needs to make sure that the message is clearly conveyed and accurately received.

▼ Practice

Make a record of your communication activities for one day. A model for organizing your record appears below.

Date: ___Tuesday, July 26_____

Communication Activity	Description of Situation
Speaking	told friend about movie I liked
Listening	listened to weather report on radio
Writing	wrote grocery list
Reading	read sports section of newspaper

Clear and Unclear Messages

Look at the two photographs on the right side of the page. In the top photograph, you can see clearly the actions of the two football players. But the bottom photograph is out of focus. The images of the players are so blurred that you can't tell what they are doing.

Sharp Image

When you receive a clear message, you have a sharp picture of the information in your mind. However, if the message is unclear, your understanding of the information is fuzzy or blurry.

Similarly, when you send a clear message, the other person knows precisely what you mean. If your message is not clear, that person may be confused.

You probably talk to many people every day, but are you really communicating? Have you ever felt frustrated because someone didn't understand what you meant to say? Do you get annoyed when the person talking to you seems rude or insensitive?

Blurry Image

Different problems can cause breakdowns in the communication process and lead to disagreement or conflict. When this happens, the sender and receiver do not share a clear understanding of the message.

▼ Practice

A. Think of a conversation in which you had a misunderstanding with another person, and analyze the situation using the questions listed below.

1. *Who* was the other person?

2. *What* was the subject of the conversation?

3. *Where* did the conversation occur?

4. *What* caused the communication breakdown?

5. *How* did these causes interfere with the communication process?

6. *What* could have solved this problem?

B. Now tell a partner about the misunderstanding.

Seeing Is Not Believing

The United States Air Force once conducted a study about UFO (unidentified flying object) sightings. The Air Force wanted to create false reports of UFOs. A plane, while flying very low, beamed a huge spotlight on the ground below. Many people who lived in the area claimed that a UFO with an intensely bright light followed them, hovered above them, and then flew away.

Of course, this so-called UFO was not a strange visitor from another planet. It was just an airplane. The people incorrectly perceived what they saw. **Perception** is the way you see and interpret the world. Two people may perceive or interpret a set of facts in different ways.

UFO or Airplane?

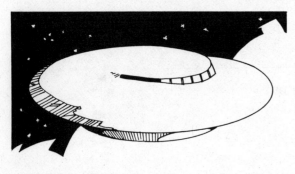 

To help you understand how you use perception, work through the following exercise.

▶ Read the two words below.

1. BATMAN   2. HERO

In the first word, did you perceive that H was the letter *A*? But in the second word, did you perceive that H was the letter *H*?

What made the difference in how you perceived the letter? The **context** of the surrounding words made the difference.

► Look at the picture below. What do you see?

Did you see rings of angels or devils? It depends on your **focus**.

► Look at the circles below. Which circle is larger?

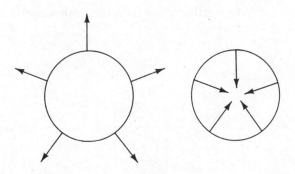

The circles are the same size. The direction of the arrows makes the circle on the left appear larger than the one on the right.

Differences in Perception

Communication involves people, and each person sees the world differently. Your background, age, experiences, and attitudes shape your perceptions. When you don't understand another person's words or feelings, the problem may be a difference in perception.

A simple story shows how attitudes and prejudices can affect communication. In one company, an office manager hired a new file clerk. The new worker was experienced and well-qualified. However, she was also tall, blonde, and very pretty. The other file clerks assumed that the office manager hired her because she was good looking. They avoided talking to her and acted unfriendly. Since they perceived her as a "dumb blond," they never got to know her. Such errors in perception unnecessarily damage communication among people.

To communicate effectively with your boss and coworkers, you should try to understand their viewpoints. You can avoid making snap judgments based on your perceptions by "putting yourself in someone else's shoes."

▼ Practice

A. Think about the conversation you described in the Practice on page 5. Try to see the misunderstanding from the other person's point of view. Write a few sentences describing how the other person felt during the disagreement. Then explain how you would handle the situation if it were to happen again.

B. Work in a small group to complete the following exercise. In the comic strip below, the characters' spoken words are omitted. Each group member should write the words that he or she thinks the characters are saying. After all of you have completed the exercise, compare your responses.

WORKING TOGETHER

Directions: This activity will help you better understand the problem of accurately sending messages to different people. Work in small groups of four people. One person in each group should get a magazine or newspaper and cut out a photograph that shows people engaged in an activity. This person should study the photograph for a few minutes without showing it to anyone else. Then follow the steps illustrated in the diagram on the left-hand side of the page.

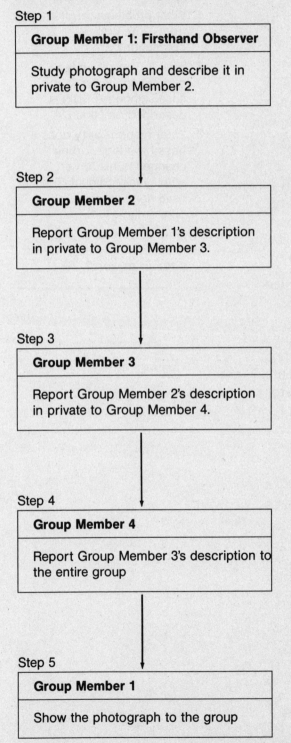

Step 1

Group Member 1: Firsthand Observer

Study photograph and describe it in private to Group Member 2.

Step 2

Group Member 2

Report Group Member 1's description in private to Group Member 3.

Step 3

Group Member 3

Report Group Member 2's description in private to Group Member 4.

Step 4

Group Member 4

Report Group Member 3's description to the entire group

Step 5

Group Member 1

Show the photograph to the group

For Discussion: After you have completed the preceding steps, discuss how the message (the description of the photograph) changed as it was passed along to each group member.

1. Which details were left out?

2. Which new details were added?

3. Which details changed?

4. What personal interpretations of the description were added?

Conclude your discussion by commenting on this statement: *Messages consist of feelings and attitudes, in addition to facts.*

I Heard It through the Grapevine

Tim is a packer at a manufacturing plant. One morning he saw a man installing a computerized machine near his work area. He thought the machine might be used to direct automated robots that packed machine parts. He started wondering if the robots would be used to replace some of the packers.

Feeling threatened, Tim shared this perception with Dolores, one of his coworkers. "Dolores," Tim said, "I bet the packing department goes automated. I can't compete with a robot. The way things look to me, I'm going to be standing in line at the unemployment office."

Dolores nodded her head in agreement. She, in turn, began circulating a rumor in the packing department about layoffs and cutbacks resulting from the new machine. Because the packers were worried about losing their jobs, their work performance started to decline.

Craig, the foreman of the packing department, learned about the rumor from Lester, another worker at the manufacturing plant. Craig then remarked, "Robots in the packing department—that's the most ridiculous thing I've ever heard of! The newly installed computer equipment is for coordinating our work with the other departments. I wonder what troublemaker started spreading that story. Those folks know that when they've got a problem, they're supposed to come to me."

▼ For Discussion

1. What problems resulted from Tim's error in perception?

2. How is Tim's mistaken perception similar to the false sightings of UFOs described on page 6?

3. What responsibility does a boss have in reporting changes to his or her employees? Should Craig have done anything differently?

4. How do you think you should react when you hear a rumor at work?

Listening Strategies

Can This Marriage Be Saved?

Dear Lorie,

I read your column every day, so I know my problem isn't unusual. I've been married for eight years and have two kids. My husband is a good father and hard worker, but he has this annoying habit of tuning me out.

Whenever I say, "I've got something to tell you," he replies, "Sure, honey, I'm all ears." Meanwhile, he looks away and gets preoccupied doing something else, like hiding his head behind the newspaper. As I'm talking, he puts on this big act of pretending to listen. He nods his head and says, "Uh-huh," "I see," or "You don't say?" All along, I know he's faking. I'll ask him a question about something I just said, and he has no idea what I'm talking about. When I call his bluff, he starts laughing and tells me it's my fault that he doesn't listen. According to him, he can't get a word in edgewise. Then I get mad at him for ignoring me. I know this may sound like a petty complaint, but it's really hurting our marriage. What should I do?

Frustrated Wife

Like the woman who wrote to Lorie, many couples need to work at communicating.

Dear Frustrated,

Many married couples have trouble communicating. Your husband has pegged you as the "talker," while he fakes his part as the "listener." In the meantime, the two of you are not really communicating with each other. Maybe you and your husband should consider seeing a marriage counselor. Good luck.

Talk About It

- Is the columnist's response helpful? What specific advice to the wife or husband could it include?
- If the husband wrote to the columnist, what do you think his letter would say?
- Have you ever felt like someone wasn't listening to you? What did you do?

How Well Do You Listen?

In the letter to the advice columnist on page 11, you read about someone with poor listening skills. Now think about conversations you've had recently and rate your own listening skills by answering *yes* or *no* to the questions below.

Listening: Self-Evaluation

	Yes	No
1. Do you find yourself daydreaming or easily distracted?	____	____
2. Do you interrupt the speaker?	____	____
3. When a point is unclear, do you feel uncomfortable asking for more information?	____	____
4. Do you look away from the person speaking to you?	____	____
5. Do you perform another activity while listening?	____	____
6. Do you pretend to pay attention to the speaker?	____	____
7. Do you stop listening when the message is too complicated?	____	____
8. Do you ignore a speaker whose behavior or appearance bothers you?	____	____

You probably answered *yes* to some of these questions. Why? Like many people, you might need to improve your listening habits. Becoming aware of your listening weaknesses is your first step in correcting them. Listening is a demanding activity that requires effort, skill, and practice.

Of course, everyone has some good listening habits as well. The lists below show one woman's listening strengths and weaknesses.

Strengths	**Weaknesses**
I look straight at the speaker.	I sometimes get distracted by people's clothes or makeup.
When I don't understand, I ask for more information.	I often interrupt other people.

▼ Practice

Jot down two specific examples of your own listening strengths and weaknesses.

Receiving the Message

Listening is an active process, not a passive one. In other words, **active listeners** concentrate on the spoken message and take responsibility for understanding what they hear. The guidelines below will help you become an active listener.

Guidelines for Active Listening

- **Focus your attention.** Resist daydreaming and ignore outside noises that may distract you. Don't think about the speaker's appearance or annoying habits. Concentrate on his or her message.

- **Identify the topic.** Ask yourself what the speaker wants you to know or do.

- **Summon up your background knowledge.** Think about what you already know about the topic. This background knowledge helps you understand new information you receive from the speaker.

- **Grasp the main ideas.** Listen for the key points of the message. To identify the key points, listen for cues from the speaker. He or she may simply say something like "My point is . . ." or "What bothered me *most* was. . . ." The speaker may also repeat or restate important ideas, say them more loudly or dramatically, or pause before and after stating them.

- **Visualize the message.** Try to form pictures in your mind of the speaker's message. You'll remember the ideas more easily if you associate them with a series of mental pictures.

- **Check your understanding.** Ask questions when you do not understand a key point. When possible, summarize the main ideas in your own words after the speaker has finished.

- **Take notes.** Jotting down the main points often helps you to understand and remember them. It is not always possible to take notes, but do so when the situation allows.

You already have experience applying some of these guidelines. For example, when you hear a news report about a hero that saved a child from a fire, you probably focus your attention automatically. You grasp the main ideas easily: Who was the hero? How did he or she get into the building and find the child? Did the child survive? and so on. You probably visualize the scene without even trying. You picture the frightened child amid flames and smoke, being handed to rescue workers under the flashing lights of fire trucks and ambulances.

▼ Practice

Listen to a radio news broadcast. Concentrate on one news story. Summon up your background knowledge—what you already know about the topic. Grasp the main idea or main point of the story. Try to visualize the story, or picture it in your mind's eye.

Check Your Understanding

As a listener, you can help a speaker make his or her message clearer. Try these listening techniques:

▼ **Communication Tip**

Ask the speaker the meaning of unfamiliar words.

- **Ask questions** when you don't understand what someone is saying. Specific questions help a speaker explain a point more clearly or completely.

- **Restate the main points in your own words** to let the speaker know you have grasped the key information. Use expressions such as *in other words*, *did you mean*, or *as I understand*.

- **Use gestures**, like nodding your head or maintaining eye contact, to indicate that you are following the conversation.

In the conversation below, notice how a bank teller and a customer use these listening techniques.

> Brenda Jones went to the bank to cash a personal check.
> The teller told her, "I'm sorry, Ms. Jones, but I can't cash your check. You have insufficient funds in your account, so your check is nonnegotiable."
> Brenda looked confused. "Could you explain what you mean by *insufficient funds* and *nonnegotiable check*?"
> The teller replied, "In other words, you don't have enough money in your account to cover the amount. The balance in your account is $50, and your check is for $220. I can't cash your check."
> Brenda nodded her head. "Oh, I see. You're telling me this check will bounce. I must have forgotten to subtract the amount of my last check. I didn't realize there wasn't enough money in my account to cash this."

► What listening skill did Brenda use?

_____

_____

_____

Brenda *asked what "non-negotiable" meant*, she *nodded her head* when she understood, and she *restated* the teller's point.

Taking Notes

Another way of staying involved in the listening process is by taking brief notes. By taking notes, you show your interest in both the speaker and the message itself. Afterward, your notes provide you with a written record of what you heard.

Many people take notes on the job. A waitress listens to customers and jots down their orders. Compare one waitress's notes to her customers' original orders:

Customer 1: I'd like a bacon, lettuce, and tomato sandwich on whole-wheat toast, no mayonnaise. Also, a cup of coffee.

Customer 2: I'd like the same.

Customer 3: I'll have the steak sandwich and a cup of coffee. Please make the steak medium rare.

Customer 4: I'll have the same, except make my steak well done.

The waitress's notes are shown at right. In writing the customers' orders, the waitress uses her own system of **abbreviations**. Similarly, you can create your own abbreviated spellings when you take notes. Listening to directions, taking phone messages, and attending meetings are all situations in which you should take notes.

▼ Note-Taking Tips

- Use your own words whenever possible.
- Use clear abbreviations.
- Jot down only the most important points.
- Reread your notes immediately and fill in any missing information.

GUEST CHECK

2 BLT on wht/
   hold the mayo
1 stk san/ MR
  " " / WD
4 cof

▼ Practice

A. Read the following conversation. Then answer the questions.

Secretary: Would you get me a ream of paper from the supply room?
Office Clerk: Sure, I'll be right back.

(10 minutes later)

Office Clerk: All the packages in the supply room were labeled *500 sheets*. I couldn't find any packages that said *reams*.
Secretary: Oh, I'm sorry. I thought you knew that a ream is a stack of 500 sheets.

1. What question should the office clerk have asked?

2. What was the result of not asking the question?

B. Call a movie theater and find out which movies are showing tonight. Take *brief* notes.

Effective Listening

Developing good listening habits will improve the way you communicate with people in your personal life. Effective listening will also help you succeed on the job. During the course of each workday, you will receive messages that test your listening skills:

- Answers to your questions

- Oral instructions

- Telephone conversations

- Discussions and meetings with coworkers

The chart below shows the results of both effective listening and poor listening. Recognizing the benefits of listening attentively in work-related situations should motivate you to continue building your skills.

On the Job	
Results of Effective Listening	Results of Poor Listening
• Get more information • Make fewer mistakes • Save time and money • Improve work relationships • Help solve problems	• Learn less about job • Make more mistakes • Waste time and money • Create misunderstandings • Cause problems

▼ Practice

A. Think about a time you encountered each of the following situations:

1. A conversation in which poor listening caused a problem

2. A conversation in which effective listening solved a problem

B. Write a paragraph describing each one. Take turns describing to each other the situations you wrote about.

WORKING TOGETHER

Directions: This activity will help you practice the listening skills you learned in this chapter. Choose a partner to work with. Each of you will take turns playing the roles of a speaker and a listener. Guidelines for both of these roles follow.

SPEAKER'S GUIDELINES

1. Think of an interesting experience from your personal life or job to tell your partner.

2. Choose a topic you can briefly explain in time order, such as an event or process.

3. Be prepared to repeat or explain a point if your partner is confused.

LISTENER'S GUIDELINES

Your goal is to understand the speaker's experience from his or her viewpoint. To reach this goal, apply these listening techniques:

1. Give the speaker your full attention.

2. Try to visualize, or picture in your mind, what the speaker is saying.

3. Jot down the main ideas, not details, of the speaker's story.

4. Avoid interrupting the speaker unnecessarily, but do ask the speaker to repeat or restate a point if you didn't understand it well enough to write it down.

5. When the speaker is finished, ask questions that show you were listening. Then restate the key points to make sure you grasped the highlights of the story.

For Discussion: After you and your partner have completed this activity, discuss this question with each other:

Which role was more demanding: speaking or listening? Why?

ON YOUR OWN

Sometimes listening at your job is difficult because of outside sounds—ringing telephones, noisy machines, other people's conversations, and so on. Simulate this situation at home. Talk to a friend or relative while the TV is on or the vacuum cleaner is running. Were you able to communicate despite the noise? Were there any communication problems?

Tuning Out the Speaker

George is a janitor for a large apartment building. Since George has occasional back trouble, the landlord hired Joe as an assistant. Joe's job is to help George with maintenance.

George: Let me give you a rundown on what you should know about the maintenance jobs for this building.

Joe: I've done janitorial work for a couple apartment buildings already, so I know what to do. I've done a little carpentry work and house painting. I'm really handy at fixing plumbing problems. I just picked that up on my own.

George: (*growing impatient*) Joe, I know you can do the job. But the landlord and the tenants like things done a certain way around here, so I just want to fill you in . . .

Joe: Some of the tenants in the building I just worked at were so picky about every little thing. During the winter, they'd call me about their apartments' being too hot or too cold. By the way, George, am I going to get calls from tenants late at night? My wife throws a fit whenever tenants call up because they've lost their keys.

George: Well, Joe, that's one of the things I need to talk to you about. Just hear me out . . .

Joe: Like I said before, George, I already know the stuff I'm supposed to do. But you probably need help lifting the garbage cans into the Dumpsters because of your bad back. Don't worry—no problem.

George: (*becoming angry*) Say, Joe, let's get one thing straight right now. When I've got something important to tell you, just listen to me until I'm finished!

Joe: OK, but you don't have to get mad about it. Now what's so important? (*Joe looks down at his shoes.*) I'm listening.

▼ **For Discussion**

1. Why did George have trouble communicating with Joe?
2. What do you think Joe should do to become a better listener?
3. Why are communication skills often as important as technical skills in doing a job well?

Speaking Strategies

Bill arrives at McDonald, Sellers & Dorfmann, a large law firm. He is interviewing for the position of messenger. The receptionist greets him politely and asks, "May I help you?"

"Yes. My name is Bill Lee, and I have a one o'clock appointment with Ms. Rivera."

"Ms. Rivera's office is on the ninth floor, suite 942. I'll telephone her, Mr. Lee, and let her know you're here." The receptionist calls Ms. Rivera's secretary and then directs Bill to the elevator. "Good luck on your interview," she says.

As Bill walks into the office suite, a woman approaches him. "Hello, I'm Joanne, Ms. Rivera's secretary. Her meeting with a client is taking longer than she expected. She should be finished in another five minutes or so. I know she's eager to talk to you. Please take a seat. She'll be with you shortly."

While Bill is waiting, he glances around the open office area, where several people are busy working. To his left, a small group of people in a glass-enclosed conference room seem to be having a lively discussion. From the office on his right, Bill overhears a lawyer dictating a

Like the employees of McDonald, Sellers & Dorfmann, these workers must speak effectively to perform their jobs.

letter to his secretary. One office worker is talking on the phone, while another is listening to a coworker's explanation of how to use the computer.

Then Bill sees a woman walking toward him. "Hello, you must be Bill Lee. I'm Sonia Rivera. Sorry to keep you waiting, but I got tied up. Well, I must say I am looking forward to discussing the messenger job with you. We're really shorthanded right now."

Bill stands up and shakes Ms. Rivera's hand. He replies, "I'm glad to meet you, Ms. Rivera. I hope we can work something out."

Talk About It

- In the story, how many people does Bill talk to? What do they talk about?
- What are the different speaking situations that Bill observes?
- Do you need to have good speaking skills on your job or for a job that you want? In which situations?

Occasions for Speaking

As you just read, Bill observed several situations in which people were speaking. Have you ever stopped to think why you speak to other people? The following reasons are probably already familiar to you.

- Sharing an experience with another person

- Commenting immediately about something you see, hear, touch, taste, or smell

- Solving a problem

- Reporting or getting information

- Asking or urging a person to do something

- Exchanging opinions or feelings

- Showing polite interest in another person

In your daily contacts with people, your ability to speak effectively is essential. For instance, you might have to explain a car problem to a mechanic, interview for a job, or attend a parent-teacher conference at your child's school.

▼ Practice

A. Read each situation below and match it with the appropriate occasion for speaking from the list above. (More than one answer may be possible.)

Example: Nellie tells Roberto that she's glad to see him back at school after his operation.
(Showing polite interest)

1. The boss tells the secretary to hold all calls.

2. Larayne tells her coworkers that she thinks "The Simpsons" is a silly show.

3. Andre tells Felicia he smells smoke in their apartment.

4. A driver asks a gas station attendant for directions.

5. Mr. and Mrs. Spencer talk about rearranging their schedules so one of them will be able to take their children to school every morning.

B. Now, jot down specific situations from your own experience that illustrate three of the occasions from the list.

An Eyewitness Account

Silently read the following eyewitness account of a hit-and-run accident, or a volunteer could read it aloud:

> Officer, I was in the parking lot when the accident occurred. I've gone over in my mind everything I saw, and I'll tell you all I remember.
>
> OK. That woman standing over there was slowly pulling out of her parking space. She was behind the wheel of the yellow Chevy. Suddenly, a gray-haired man driving a new red BMW came speeding down the lane. I bet he was going about 35 miles per hour. He obviously didn't notice the Chevy backing up because he didn't slow down.
>
> Next, I heard metal crunching as the BMW scraped against the Chevy. The gray-haired man slowed down for a second to check out the damage to the other car. Then he gunned his motor and raced out of the lot. I caught a glimpse of his license plate—CS 21 is all I can remember. Are there any other questions you'd like to ask me?

This eyewitness's account was effective because he or she

- had something worthwhile to say

- supported his or her observations with relevant details

- organized the message so the officer could easily follow it

- used language the officer could understand

Now read another eyewitness account of the same accident. (A different volunteer could read this aloud.)

> Officer, I'm telling you that guy in the red sports car was driving like a maniac. He was speeding down the lane like he was racing in the Indy 500 or something. That car was moving so fast, the license plate number was just a blur. He probably left in such a hurry because he doesn't have insurance. That poor lady in the Chevy or Buick or whatever is going to get stuck paying for the damages.

In contrast to the first eyewitness, the second does not provide the police officer with useful information.

▶ Why is the second eyewitness account less helpful? What information did this witness leave out?

Sending the Message

How do you tell jokes or stories? What speaking techniques do you use to hold the listener's attention? After you've described an experience, has the listener ever asked you, "So what's the point?" All the speaking skills you use in your personal conversations can also apply at work.

As you learned earlier, both the speaker and the listener are responsible for making sure a message is understood. The speaker's role in the communication process is sending the message to the listener. The diagram below further details these two roles.

The circle on the left lists a series of steps the speaker should follow. For your casual conversations, you may not need to plan your spoken message carefully. At work, however, you will be judged by your ability to communicate effectively, so a more structured approach to speaking situations will be helpful. The steps for sending clear messages are explained in more detail on the next page.

The Communication Exchange

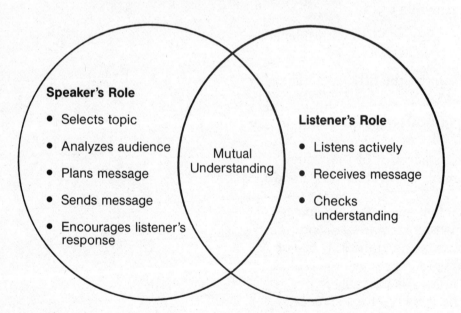

Speaker's Role

- Selects topic
- Analyzes audience
- Plans message
- Sends message
- Encourages listener's response

Mutual Understanding

Listener's Role

- Listens actively
- Receives message
- Checks understanding

Strategies for Effective Speaking

Step 1: Select your topic. Identify *what* you want to talk about. What do you want the listener to know or do?

Step 2: Analyze your audience. Determine what the listener already knows about the topic. Think about the listener's past experience and about previous conversations the two of you may have had. Understanding the listener will help you adapt your choice of words and your explanation of details to match the listener's knowledge of your topic.

Step 3: Plan the message. Decide what main points you need to make. Find a clear order in which to present them.

Step 4: Send the message. Speak at a comfortable rate. Maintain eye contact so the listener knows you are concerned that he or she is getting the message. Emphasize key points: repeat or restate them, pause, or use signal expressions such as *First*, *In addition*, or *It's important to know that.* . . . Check your listener's understanding: observe the listener's face and gestures and accept his or her questions.

Step 5: Encourage the listener's response. Invite the listener to ask questions or to comment on the message.

▼ Practice

Reread the first eyewitness account on page 21. Then answer the questions below.

1. What is the speaker's topic?

2. Who is the speaker's audience?

3. Did the speaker plan the message? Give a reason for your answer.

4. How is the message organized?

5. How does the eyewitness encourage a response?

Talking with Coworkers

In the '70s comedy series "The Mary Tyler Moore Show," the cast of characters in the newsroom behaves like a close-knit family. All the employees share their personal experiences with one another. Lou Grant, the boss, is like a father. The producer, the newswriter, and the anchorman ask Lou's advice about marriage, dating, and other private matters. Stories about their problems are often funny.

In real life, however, the employee relationships shown on "The Mary Tyler Moore Show" are not an ideal model to follow. More than likely you will become close friends with some of your coworkers. Working with people you trust and like makes your job more enjoyable. However, developing friendships takes time, and you should be careful about what you say to coworkers before you know them very well.

There are many occasions for social conversations at your job—coffee breaks, lunch breaks, or company parties. When chatting with other employees, follow these guidelines.

- **Choose appropriate topics of conversation.** You should not discuss personal problems in detail at your job. As a rule, try to separate your private life from your professional life. Also, you should consider beforehand whether or not a certain topic of conversation will hurt or offend someone.

- **Avoid gossip.** Gossiping about coworkers damages work relationships and may cause others to lose respect for you. Generally, gossip consists of distorted, inaccurate messages.

- **Speak politely to your coworkers regardless of your personal feelings.** Just as there are people you will like at your job, there will be people you will dislike. Your conversations should not reveal any negative feelings you may have about another employee.

Directions: Choose a partner to work with. Each of you will take turns playing the roles of speaker and listener. Guidelines for both of these roles follow.

SPEAKER'S GUIDELINES

Briefly describe to your partner your current job or a job you would like to have. Your description should detail the skills and responsibilities needed to perform the job well. For example, a telephone salesperson should have a pleasant speaking voice, the ability to persuade others, and selling experience. To speak effectively, follow this procedure:

1. **Select your topic.** Decide which job you will describe. Focus on providing factual information, rather than personal feelings, about the job.

2. **Analyze your audience.** Ask yourself how much your partner probably knows about your topic already. You may need to give some background information.

3. **Plan the message.** You may want to jot down key points in the order you want to say them.

4. **Send the message.** Use language the listener understands. Emphasize important points. Maintain eye contact and look for signs of understanding or confusion. Respond to the listener's questions.

5. **Encourage the listener's response.** Invite questions or comments about your message.

LISTENER'S GUIDELINES

Your role is to listen actively. Focus on your partner's message and ask questions if the message is unclear. (You may want to review the guidelines for active listening on page 13.) Afterward, evaluate the speaker's performance by answering the following questions:

1. What did the speaker do to hold your attention?

2. Was the speaker's message easy to follow?

3. Did the speaker pay attention to your reactions? How could you tell?

4. Did the speaker respond to your questions? How?

For Discussion: After you and your partner complete the activity, compare your evaluations of each other. Discuss ways you might improve both your speaking and listening skills.

The Lunch Break

Denise and Sheila are salesclerks at a large discount chain store. They are friendly at work but never see each other socially. Denise is very talkative, while Sheila is quiet and shy. As they are eating in the employee cafeteria, they have the following conversation:

Denise: You know Lisa, the cashier in the cosmetics department, is really getting on my nerves. She's always in a bad mood in the morning. Whenever I say hello to her, she gives me a dirty look or just turns her head like I was invisible or something. That woman has a real problem, and I bet I know what it is.

Sheila: She seems all right to me. (*trying to change the subject*) The roast beef is really good today.

Denise: Anyway, my neighbor used to date Lisa. She dropped him because he didn't spend enough money on her. She just uses people.

Sheila: Like I said before, Denise, I don't have a problem with Lisa. And besides . . .

Denise: Well, I do. Sure, she puts a smile on her face for the customers and the boss. But I can see right through that act, even though the boss obviously falls for it. Why do you think she got promoted to head cashier of the cosmetics department? She's always flattering the boss and bragging about how many sales she makes.

▼ For Discussion

1. How is Denise, the speaker, insensitive to Sheila, the listener?

2. What topics of conversation should not be discussed with coworkers?

3. What would you do if someone at your job started gossiping about one of your coworkers?

4. How are work friends different from personal friends?

Nonverbal Communication

Look at the pictures on this page. Each person is communicating **nonverbally**—that is, without speaking.

Message: "Stop!"

Message: "Strike!"

Talk About It

- Can you think of any other nonverbal signals used in sports? Describe one signal and its meaning.
- What gestures do people commonly use to:
  - say goodbye?
  - beckon to a child?
  - get a waitress's attention?
  - show they don't know something?

Unspoken Messages

The pictures on page 27 show people communicating nonverbally. This means their gestures and body positions convey messages without using words.

You also "speak" with your body. Your facial expressions, gestures, and posture are a silent language, revealing your feelings and attitudes.

Nonverbal communication may reinforce a spoken message. Actors, for instance, learn how to use facial expressions, gestures, and body movements that enhance the lines they speak. Nonverbal communication may also act as a substitute for the words themselves. Roger Ebert and Gene Siskel, two well-known film critics, use hand gestures to rate movies. "Thumbs up" indicates a good movie, while "thumbs down" signals a bad movie.

Study each picture below, paying attention to the nonverbal communication.

Remember, however, that most nonverbal messages are open to interpretation. A man might shrug his shoulders because he has a sore muscle. A woman might squint because she has forgotten to wear her glasses. No gesture or facial expression has a single, precise meaning. Try to "read" another person's nonverbal communication in the context of a particular situation.

A person's message comes across most clearly when the spoken words match the accompanying nonverbal communication. For instance, if a coworker says, "Sure, I have plenty of time to talk," while turning his back to you, his message is not clear.

Spoken Message: "I'm confused" or "I disagree."

Nonverbal Communication: shrugging shoulders, shaking head from side to side, glancing away, squinting eyes, wrinkling forehead

Spoken Message: "I'm going to be late."

Nonverbal Communication: looking at watch, frowning

▼ Practice

A. Based on your observations, write some common nonverbal signals associated with each spoken message shown below. Use the examples on page 28 as a model.

1. **Spoken Message:** "I'm surprised!"

   Nonverbal Communication: _____

   _____

2. **Spoken Message:** "I'm angry."

   Nonverbal Communication: _____

   _____

3. **Spoken Message:** "I'm busy."

   Nonverbal Communication: _____

   _____

B. Choose a partner to work with. Each of you will take turns playing the roles of speaker and listener. Guidelines for both of these roles follow.

Speaker's Guidelines: Imagine that you just won $5 million in your state lottery. Describe to your partner your emotional reactions and your plans for spending the money. Also, explain how winning the lottery will change your life.

Listener's Guidelines: Your role is to notice how your partner's nonverbal communication corresponds to his or her spoken message. As your partner is talking, jot down your observations of the following:

- facial expressions
- gestures
- body position
- tone of voice

When your partner is finished, tell him or her your observations. Then invite your partner to respond to your comments.

Showing Your Attitude

Your attitude toward your job will be judged in part by your nonverbal communication. Ideally, your nonverbal behavior at work should express confidence, interest, and eagerness. Here are some common sense do's and don'ts. See if you can add one or two items to each list.

- DO make eye contact.
- DO assume a pleasant facial expression.
- DO sit up straight and lean forward slightly.

_____

_____

- DON'T slouch.
- DON'T put your feet up.
- DON'T smack or crack chewing gum.
- DON'T sigh loudly.

_____

_____

Of course, in attempting to send positive signals, you can go overboard. If you stare at the other person without _ever_ looking away, you will make him or her uncomfortable. If you smile and nod too much, you will appear weak or insincere. Be sure your nonverbal signals are positive but appropriate.

▼ Practice

Read this story and answer the questions that follow.

Janine, a teacher's aide, was attending a staff meeting at the child-care center. The director had been speaking for twenty minutes about the center's plan to reorganize the play areas. Janine was excited about the plan and was eager to get to work. However, she felt the director was wasting time explaining and justifying every step of the plan.

Janine slouched lower in her seat and put one foot up on an empty chair. She examined her fingernails and began to pick at the nail polish on her thumb. As the director talked on, Janine looked at her watch, raised her eyebrows, and sighed loudly.

1. What nonverbal signals did Janine send? Describe her expressions, gestures, and body positions.

2. How do you think the director interpreted Janine's nonverbal signals?

3. Did Janine's nonverbal communication truly reflect her overall attitude toward the job? Explain.

4. How might Janine have nonverbally communicated a more positive attitude during the meeting?

Directions: This activity will help increase your awareness of your own and other people's nonverbal behavior. Choose a partner to work with. Each partner will take turns playing the role of speaker and listener. Afterward, you will discuss your reactions. Guidelines for both of the roles follow.

SPEAKER'S GUIDELINES
Describe your neighborhood to your partner. (If you live in the same neighborhood, you may describe your block.) Tell about the people who live there, the buildings, the streets, the parks, the shopping facilities, and the businesses. Tell what you like and dislike about your neighborhood.

LISTENER'S GUIDELINES
Before you listen to the speaker, decide whether to send *positive* nonverbal signals or *negative* ones. Use body language and be consistent about sending positive or negative signals as the speaker talks.

For Discussion: When you are finished playing your roles, discuss the speaker's reactions to the listener's nonverbal communication.

Does this woman's nonverbal communication convey a positive or negative attitude?

ON YOUR OWN
Watch a television talk show. Turn off the sound and focus your attention on the participants' body language. Then, turn the sound back on and pay attention to both the verbal and nonverbal communication.

Late Again

Sue is an order taker at a fast-food chain restaurant. She works from 5:30 A.M. to 11 A.M.—the breakfast shift. For the last week, she has been 10 to 20 minutes late for work. This morning she arrives at 5:45. Rick, the manager, meets her at the door. His hands are folded across his chest and he is frowning. "Sue," he says in an angry tone of voice, "come with me."

Rick escorts Sue to his office. "Sit down," he says coldly. Sue clutches the arms of the chair tightly and swings her right foot back and forth.

Rick opens his desk drawer and pulls out Sue's time sheet. He studies the time sheet and pushes it across the desk toward Sue. "Well?" he says. Sue looks away and stares at the floor. "Look at me. You *should* be rested enough," Rick adds sarcastically. "After all, you obviously get more sleep than any other employee working the breakfast shift."

▼ **For Discussion**

1. What nonverbal communication takes place between Rick and Sue? How does it prevent them from speaking to each other in a straightforward manner?

2. Do you think Rick handled the situation well? Why or why not?

3. Let's assume Sue had a good reason for being late. How should she have handled the situation differently?

Are You Listening?

Carl was busy bagging groceries for a home delivery when the next customer said to him, "I'd like my groceries in large, double-paper bags. Also, please put the meat in freezer bags."

Carl nodded his head in agreement. "Sure, ma'am, no problem," he replied, even though he hadn't paid any attention to what she had said. He was still preoccupied with the previous order.

Carl began packing her groceries in plastic bags. The customer said, "Excuse me, young man, I just told you I wanted double-paper bags, not plastic bags."

Carl rolled his eyes and shook his head. "Sorry, ma'am. Most customers prefer the plastic bags. Anything you say," he smirked. Carl looked annoyed as he corrected his mistake.

▼ **For Discussion**

1. How did Carl's behavior contradict his spoken words?

2. How do you think the customer reacted to Carl's gestures and facial expressions?

3. How could Carl have handled this situation more positively?

Following Directions

Daryl was mowing the lawn in his backyard. His mother, Sondra, was in the living room watching TV when suddenly she heard Daryl yell. He came running into the house, holding his arm and shouting, "A bee just stung me!" She told him to calm down and sit in the easy chair. "Don't worry—I'll get help," she said.

She remembered that the phone book had listings of tape-recorded first-aid instructions. She found "First Aid for Bee Stings" and dialed the number. Ignoring the TV and Daryl's exclamations of pain, she listened carefully to the tape recording. It began:

"You are listening to Tape 461: First Aid for Bee Stings. Follow these steps to relieve pain and swelling."

As Sondra listened, she pictured each step in her mind.

"First, remove the stinger by gently rubbing it with a soft cloth. Next, wrap ice in a wet cloth and apply it to the bee sting. Tell the person to sit or lie down."

"If the bee sting is on the arm or leg, the person should hang his arm or leg down. Tie a towel or band of cloth snugly around the arm or leg, just above the bee sting. Make sure the band is not too tight. After five minutes, remove the band entirely. These instructions will be repeated one more time."

Sondra already had a sheet of paper and a pen handy. She listened carefully to the repeated instructions and took notes.

> 1. remove stinger - rub gently with cloth
> 2. ice wrapped in cloth on sting
> 3. keep him in chair
> 4. hang arm down
> 5. tie towel around arm above sting - not too tight
> 6. remove band after 5 minutes

Sondra followed the instructions step by step. Shortly after, Daryl felt much better.

Talk About It

- How did Sondra focus her attention?

- What two techniques did Sondra use to help herself understand and remember the steps?

Visualizing Instructions

When you need to follow instructions, your first task is to focus your attention. Then, as you listen, it helps to visualize the instructions. If you get a clear mental picture of each step, it will be easier to remember and carry out the instructions correctly.

▼ Practice

A. Your instructor will read aloud the first-aid instructions for treating bee stings (page 33). Or, go back and reread the instructions yourself. As you listen or read, *picture each step in your mind*. Then, with a partner, act out the first-aid treatment. Take turns playing the roles of bee-sting victim and helper.

B. One person should read aloud the following series of steps. The rest of the class will follow the reader's step-by-step instructions. If you are not working with a class, read the instructions yourself. As you listen, or read, picture each step in your mind and perform the action.

Reader: Listen to these instructions. I will pause briefly after each step so you can complete it.

Step 1: Take out a sheet of paper.
Step 2: Print your name and address in the upper left-hand corner.
Step 3: Underline your name.
Step 4: Circle your address.
Step 5: Draw a small square in the upper right-hand corner and put a check mark inside it.
Step 6: Draw a large circle in the center of your paper.
Step 7: Draw two lines to divide the circle into four equal parts. One line should go from the top to the bottom. The other line should go from the left-hand side to the right-hand side.
Step 8: In the top right segment of the circle, print the word *listening* in lower-case letters, not capital letters.
Step 9: In the bottom right segment of the circle, print the word *speaking* in lower-case letters.
Step 10: In the top left segment, print the word *reading* in lower-case letters.
Step 11: In the bottom left segment, print the word *writing* in lower-case letters.
Step 12: Underneath the circle, print the word *communication* in capital letters.

Instructions in Everyday Life

You have read how Sondra relied on her listening skills to handle a medical emergency. Like Sondra, you already have experience listening to directions.

The instructions you listened to as a child were fairly simple. For example, someone probably told you how to use a pair of scissors, how to play a game, or how to set the table.

However, many of the instructions you listen to as an adult are more complex. How did you learn how to drive a car? How did you learn how to obtain a money order? Somebody probably gave you spoken directions and guided you through a series of steps.

▶ What have you learned to do by following oral instructions? Write four activities or tasks on the lines below. Some other examples follow.

_____

_____

_____

_____

Examples of Adult Tasks and Activities

- operating a cash register
- making lasagna
- fixing a leaky faucet
- using a sewing machine

- changing a flat tire
- following a route to someone's house
- playing a card game
- hooking up stereo speakers

▼ Practice

Read about how Rita learned to use her new ATM (automated teller machine) card. Then answer the questions that follow the dialog.

Rita's bank mailed her an ATM card, but she was unsure how to use it. She went to a nearby grocery store that had an automated teller machine. She thought the directions on the machine were confusing. Then she saw a note taped on the machine: "If you are having problems using this machine, ask the store manager for assistance." Rita approached the store manager and the following conversation took place.

Rita: Could you show me how to use the ATM? I've never used one before.

Store Manager: Sure, I'd be glad to help you. Some people are afraid of the machine at first because it's a computer. But, really, it's easy to use and very convenient. Here, let me show you. The first thing you do is insert your Cash Station card in this slot face up.

Rita: I just feed it in like this?

Store Manager: That's right. When the red light goes on, enter your PIN.

Rita: What's a PIN?

Store Manager: Your personal identification number.

Rita: Oh, yeah. That's my secret code of four numbers.

Store Manager: Exactly. I'll turn my head, and you hit the four numbers on the keyboard.

Rita: OK, I'm done. What's the next step?

Store Manager: Enter the amount of your withdrawal transaction. In other words, enter how much money you want—$20, $40, $100—then hit two extra zeros to go after the decimal point.

Rita: OK, I want $40, so I'll hit the 4 and three zeros on the keyboard.

Store Manager: Right. Now your transaction is being processed. Slip this sheet of paper called a Transaction Record in the slot. This is a kind of receipt. Right now the computer is typing the day and time of your checking withdrawal, plus your amount. Now lift the top of the drawer, and you'll find $40.

Rita: Here it is! Thanks a lot.

Listed below are the basic steps for withdrawing money from an Automated Teller Machine. However, the steps are arranged in jumbled order. Number the steps 1 through 5 to show the correct sequence.

_____ Place the Transaction Record slip in the correct slot.

_____ Enter your PIN on the keyboard.

_____ Open the drawer and remove your money.

_____ Insert your Cash Station card in the slot.

_____ Enter the amount of money on the keyboard.

Following a Procedure

In the preceding exercise, Rita learned how to follow a **procedure**—a series of step-by-step instructions. Similarly, much of your on-the-job training consists of listening to instructions and observing procedures.

Listening to Learn a Procedure

- **Focus your attention.** Screen out distractions and control daydreaming.

- **Identify the topic.** Find out the procedure to be explained.

- **Summon up your background knowledge.** Keep in mind what you may already know about the procedure.

- **Grasp the main ideas.** Be sure you hear and understand each step of the procedure.

- **Listen for the order of the steps.** Usually, the speaker will present the steps in the order in which they must be done. The speaker will use words like *First* and *Next* as signals. However, some steps may be presented out of order. Be especially alert when the speaker says something like "Before you do this step, you should . . ." or "Do not complete this step unless you have . . ."

- **Visualize the message.** As you listen, try to picture each step of the procedure. Often the speaker will actually demonstrate the process. In this case, try to form and store away mental pictures of the demonstration.

- **Check your understanding.** Ask questions when you are not sure you understand a step. When you have heard all the instructions, restate them in your own words.

- **Take notes.** Whenever possible, briefly jot down the steps of the procedure and any points the speaker emphasizes.

▼ Practice

Luis is the head of the mail room. He gave Wayne, the new mail-room clerk, the following information. Listen as your instructor reads it aloud. Then answer the questions.

> "Wayne, one of your duties is to process incoming mail. Always sort the morning mail as soon as you get to work. First, sort the mail by department—accounting department, purchasing department, word-processing department, et cetera. Then go through the stack of mail for each department and pull the envelopes marked *special delivery* and *certified mail*. Sort them according to the two categories and put a rubber band around each type of letter. Then place the special delivery and certified mail envelopes on top of the stack for the right department."

Listening exercise

1. What is the topic of Luis's instructions?

2. What steps should Wayne follow? Briefly write them down in the correct sequence.

Taking Notes on Instructions

Notes provide you with a written record of the information you have received. For example, Sondra's notes on page 33 summarized a step-by-step procedure. Referring to them enabled her to perform the procedure accurately—treating Daryl's bee sting. Similarly, you should also take notes when you are listening to oral directions, particularly for procedures consisting of several steps. Then you can refer to your written set of instructions when necessary.

In the workplace, your note-taking procedure should go a few steps further than Sondra's emergency note taking. Whenever possible, you'll want to check your notes with the speaker and make corrections.

Use the following note-taking tips as a guide:

- Use your own words whenever you can.

- Use clear abbreviations.

- Number the steps in the exact order you are to follow them.

- Whenever possible, check the accuracy of your notes by reading the key steps aloud to your speaker.

- Add missing information and correct errors.

- Make a final copy of the notes for your own reference.

▼ Practice

A supervisor is telling a new hotel employee how to open the doors of the guest rooms. Your instructor will read aloud the supervisor's instructions below and will then repeat the reading. Listen and take notes, numbering each step of the procedure. Reread your notes and then check them against the supervisor's written instructions. (If you are not working with a class, read the instructions.)

> "We don't use keys anymore for security reasons. Burglars know how to pick locks, so we've got this new procedure. Next to the door of each room you'll see a slot with a small light above it. Insert this small plastic card into the slot. Hold it in place for a moment until the light goes on and you hear a buzzer. Immediately push down the door handle, and remove the card from the slot. You may have to practice a few times to get the timing right. Make sure you can do it easily so you can demonstrate the process to the guests."

WORKING TOGETHER

Directions: Choose a partner to work with. Each of you will take turns playing the roles of a trainer and a trainee. Guidelines for both of these roles follow.

TRAINER'S GUIDELINES

Think of a task or an activity that you know how to do very well. For example, you might choose one of the tasks or activities you listed on page 35. Then teach the task or activity to your partner, the trainee:

1. Briefly describe the task.

2. Explain the steps in performing the task.

3. Clearly state each step in the correct sequence.

4. If necessary, repeat your instructions from start to finish.

As you are giving the instructions, maintain eye contact with your partner. This will help you gauge how well he or she understands your directions. Be sure to draw attention to important points, repeating them if necessary so your partner can write them down.

TRAINEE'S GUIDELINES

Your role is to learn a task or activity. Listen carefully to your partner's instructions:

1. Focus your attention.

2. Identify the topic. What task will you learn to do?

3. Summon up your background knowledge. Do you know anything about the task already? Keep this in mind as you listen to your partner's instructions. Be aware, however, that your partner may describe a procedure different from the one you are familiar with.

4. Visualize the procedure.

5. Take notes. Jot down the main steps of the task in the correct sequence.

6. Check your understanding. Ask questions as necessary while you are receiving the instructions. Afterward, restate the instructions in your own words. Use your notes as a reference.

7. If possible, actually perform the task or act it out.

For Discussion: After you and your partner have completed the activity, evaluate each others' instructions. Answer these questions:

1. Were the instruction easy to follow? Why or why not?

2. What, if anything, could have made the instructions clearer?

The Dishwasher Who Wouldn't Listen

Carol was just hired as a kitchen helper for a large restaurant. Her main job is washing dishes. Dora, Carol's coworker, is in charge of training her.

Dora: You'll have to buy shoes with rippled rubber soles. The kitchen floor gets wet and slippery.

Carol: Those shoes cost a lot of money. Can't I just wear gym shoes?

Dora: No. If you want to work here, you have to wear the right shoes. Whether you can afford them or not isn't my problem. Now let me explain the dishwashing job. The busboys put the dishes in shallow plastic bins with slits on the bottom. The busboys sort all the dishes— glassware, dinner plates, bowls, and so on. They stack the bins on this long counter next to the sink. Then the first thing you do is . . .

Carol: Rinse the bowls?

Dora: No, you rinse the bowls last. Now don't interrupt me until I'm finished. Where was I? Oh, yeah, the first thing you do is rinse the glassware. Drag the bin filled with glassware to the sink. Rinse each glass with this spray gun next to the faucet. Then turn all the glasses upside down. Pick up the bin of glasses and slide it onto the conveyor belt on the other side of the sink. The conveyor belt carries the bins to the dishwashing system. It works kind of like a car wash. Oh, I forgot to tell you something. You have to wear . . .

Carol: I know, shoes with rubber soles.

Dora: Stop finishing my sentences for me. You have to wear rubber gloves. Now do you have any questions so far?

Carol: Yes, I was wondering if the waitresses and the busboys give us part of their tips.

Dora: You know, Carol, you have a real attitude problem. I meant do you understand how to wash the glassware?

Carol: Sure, it's easy. I have to wear rubber gloves while I hold the glasses upside down and rinse them with a spray gun.

▼ For Discussion

1. What advice would you give Carol on listening to oral instructions?
2. How could Carol and Dora improve the communication between them?
3. If you were Carol, what notes might you write down about the dishwashing job?

▼ Interview Activity

Interview two people you know about their jobs. Ask them what they do when they are listening to instructions. Share the results of the interviews with the rest of the class.

Asking Questions

Steve went to the local hardware store to return an electric power drill he had bought for his son. "I'd like a refund, please," he told the clerk.

"Do you have the receipt?" the store clerk asked.

"No, I threw it away. I bought the drill as a gift. I didn't realize my son already had one."

"Sorry, sir, our policy is no refunds or exchanges without a sales receipt," the clerk said.

Some shoppers, like Steve, assume they will not have a problem returning the merchandise they buy. To avoid this problem, the Better Business Bureau (BBB) offers the following tips to shoppers.

The customer service desk handles refunds.

It is important to remember that refunds or exchanges are voluntarily provided by stores with which you may do business. They are privileges, not rights. When you make purchasing decisions, a store's policy concerning refunds or exchanges is a consideration you should keep in mind.

When shopping, check the following:

- Does the store have an exchange policy? Will they give refunds, or will they credit your account or supply a credit slip?
- For a refund or exchange, will you need a sales receipt?
- Is there a time limit for returning the merchandise? If so, is it also applicable to gift items?
- Will the store accept return of personal apparel (such as nightgowns)?
- Does the store have a policy of "satisfaction guaranteed" or your money back?

Ask these questions before you make your next purchase.

Talk About It

- Describe a situation in which you returned or exchanged merchandise. Was there a problem? If so, why?
- How do the BBB questions help you shop wisely?

A Game of Asking Questions

Have you ever watched "Jeopardy," the TV game show? A contestant selects a category, such as movie stars, TV shows, sports, geography, and so on. The host gives the contestant a clue about a specific topic in that category. The contestant must identify the topic in the form of a question. Here are some examples:

Category: Football
Host: This NFL team won the 1986 Super Bowl.
Contestant: Who are the Chicago Bears?

Category: TV Shows
Host: This night-time soap opera focuses on the Ewing family's problems and business deals.
Contestant: What is "Dallas"?

Category: Food
Host: This Italian pasta dish is made with layers of broad noodles, tomato sauce, ground meat, and cheese.
Contestant: What is lasagna?

Asking the correct questions shows the contestant's knowledge of the information given.

▼ Practice

Now you'll get a chance to play "Jeopardy". Choose one of the categories listed below or think of your own topic.

football	food	TV shows
baseball	cars	TV characters
basketball	games	movies
famous athletes	machines	movie stars

Write down a topic, a "Jeopardy"-type statement about the topic, and the corresponding answer in the form of a question. The answer should begin with the words *who* or *what*. Use the examples on this page as a model.

As a class activity, or with a partner, play an informal version of "Jeopardy." Take turns reading topics and related statements. Whoever knows the answer should say it in the form of a question, beginning with the words *who* or *what*.

Getting Information

When you listen to a news story on the radio or TV, you can find the most important points by asking questions beginning with the five Ws—the words *who, what, when, where,* and *why.*

▶ A volunteer should read the news broadcast below. Listen carefully. Answer the questions that follow.

> The City Council of Monroeville passed a law Wednesday prohibiting city residents from keeping pit bulls as pets. One alderman remarked, "Pit bulls are a public menace. We need to prevent attacks from these vicious dogs."

▼ **Communication Tip**

You can usually judge the effectiveness of your question by the response. A good question generally produces a good answer.

1. Who passed a law? _____
2. What law was passed? _____
3. When was it passed? _____
4. Where was it passed? _____
5. Why was it passed? _____

Compare your answers to the ones below.

1. the City Council
2. a law prohibiting pit bulls as pets
3. Wednesday
4. Monroeville
5. to protect people against attacks

Similarly, asking questions beginning with the five Ws, as well as the word *how,* can help you get the facts you need.

▼ Practice

A. Suppose you needed to hire a babysitter. Write five questions you would ask during an interview with a babysitter.

B. Imagine you are looking at an apartment that you might rent. Write five questions you would ask the landlord before making a decision.

Asking Specific Questions

In your personal conversations, you probably ask questions automatically. You may ask vague questions, such as "How's that?" or "Would you run that by me again?"

At your job, however, you will need to build your skills in asking specific questions. For example, even if you listen carefully to directions, you still may not get all the information you need. Your boss or coworkers may give you incomplete instructions or use words you don't understand. You can clear up any confusion immediately by preparing good questions:

- Pinpoint what you need to know.

- Word your questions precisely to get the information you need.

Particularly if you are a new employee, you will have many questions about your job. When this is the case, follow this plan for getting information:

- Prepare your questions in advance—write them down if necessary.

- Choose the best-qualified person to answer your questions.

- Be considerate of the other person's work responsibilities. Ask that person to schedule a convenient time to talk.

▼ Practice

Carla is a new employee and is eager to do a good job. Because she's unsure of her job responsibilities, she frequently barges into her boss's office and blurts out a question. The boss thinks she's a nuisance rather than an overly conscientious worker. What steps should Carla take to change her boss's perception of her? Refer to the guidelines above.

_____

_____

_____

_____

WORKING TOGETHER

Directions: This activity will help you practice asking questions to get information. Choose a partner to work with. Both of you will take turns interviewing each other. The interview will give you the opportunity to know one of your classmates better. Guidelines for the interviewer and the interviewee follow.

INTERVIEWER'S GUIDELINES

Think of some general topics, such as the ones shown below. Then prepare specific questions related to the topics. Use the diagram below to help you organize the questions for your interview.

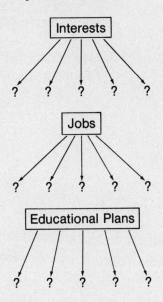

1. Prepare several questions for each topic in advance. Decide what you want to know. Don't ask questions that are too personal.

2. Ask questions using the words *who, what, when, where, why,* and *how.* Avoid asking too many questions that can be answered with a simple *yes* or *no.*

3. As you ask each question, allow your partner the time to give a complete response. Don't interrupt your partner.

4. If your partner's answer seems unclear, reword your question. When you have finished interviewing your partner, summarize what you have learned about him or her.

INTERVIEWEE'S GUIDELINES

1. Listen carefully to each question. Determine exactly what the interviewer wants to know. You may want to restate some of the questions in your own words as a way of checking your understanding.

2. If necessary, take time to respond. Think about what you want to say and the clearest way to say it. Don't give information unrelated to the question.

ON YOUR OWN

Watch a talk show on TV. Jot down some questions that the host of the show asks the guest. If you were a member of the studio audience, what questions would you ask the guest?

The Mix-Up

Leslie is an office assistant at an insurance company. She works hard and always completes her assigned tasks on time. However, Leslie is very shy and feels uncomfortable talking to her boss, Ted. She avoids asking him questions because she's afraid she will sound foolish.

One morning Ted told Leslie, "Please deliver this memo to Donald Jackson right away. I have an important meeting with him in a couple of hours. He needs to review the memo before the meeting."

After Leslie left his office, she realized that there were two men named Donald Jackson working at the insurance company. One worked in the Personnel Department and the other worked in the Legal Department. She decided to give the memo to Donald Jackson in Personnel, since he and her boss had frequent meetings.

When Leslie returned to her workspace, Ted was waiting for her. His arms were folded and he was scowling. "That memo was supposed to go to Donald Jackson in the Legal Department. It had confidential information."

Say What?

Ed is a new employee at an auto parts factory. Henry, his coworker, is explaining the parking lot policy.

Henry: The foreman told me that sometimes you'll be driving to work. You'll need to fill out the parking lot form. Ask Clara in the main office for the form. She'll give you an employee sticker to put on your windshield. You can park anywhere in the lot except in the spots marked HANDICAPPED PARKING ONLY and VISITORS ONLY.
Ed: Could you run that by me again?
Henry: Do you mean you want me to repeat the whole thing?
Ed: No. Does each employee have a reserved spot?
Henry: No, I just told you that you can park anywhere except for the specially reserved parking spaces.

▼ **For Discussion**
1. What should you do if you're unsure about your boss's directions?
2. Why do you need accurate information before making a decision?
3. How do you think Leslie responded to Ted when he confronted her?

▼ **For Discussion**
1. Was Ed listening carefully? How do his questions reveal that he wasn't paying close attention?
2. Why is it important to ask the speaker specific questions?

Giving Directions

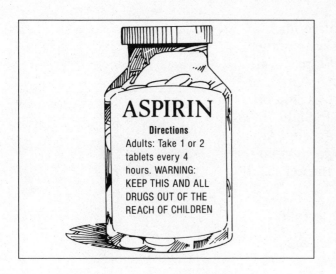

ASPIRIN

Directions
Adults: Take 1 or 2
tablets every 4
hours. WARNING:
KEEP THIS AND ALL
DRUGS OUT OF THE
REACH OF CHILDREN

VEGETABLE
SOUP

Directions
DO NOT ADD WATER
1. Pour contents into pan.
2. Stir for 5 minutes
while heating on low
flame.
3. Serve.

BEAUTY MAGIC
HAIR SPRAY

Directions
Hold can 8
inches from
hair. Press
pump using
quick strokes.
CAUTION:
CONTENTS
FLAMMABLE.

CLEAN SHAVE

Directions
1. Wet skin.
2. Shake can.
3. Press tip to
release lather.
4. Apply to skin.
5. Shave.
6. Rinse skin with
water after shaving.

Talk About It

- Why are these panel instructions easy to understand?
- Find examples of precautions and warnings on these labels. Why are such precautions or warnings important?
- Look in your book bag, briefcase, or purse for a product that lists directions on its label. How are the steps of the directions organized? What precautions or warnings are included?

Being Clear

Nelson needed directions. He stopped a woman on the street and said, "Excuse me. I'm from out of town. Could you tell me how to get to the Silver Screen Theater?"

The woman replied, "Keep going a few blocks or so until you get to a busy intersection. There's a bus stop on that corner. I'm pretty sure one of those buses will take you in the vicinity of the Silver Screen Theater."

Nelson was confused because the woman's directions were so vague. He continued walking and asked another woman for directions to the theater. She told him, "Walk north for three blocks until you get to the intersection of Spruce Street and Kenton Avenue. There's a bus stop on the—let's see—southwest corner next to the stoplight. Take bus number 141 heading east down Kenton Avenue. After a couple of miles, the bus will pull into a large shopping center called Terrace Mall. That's where the theater is. I'll draw you a map."

Nelson found these directions clear and easy to follow.

▶ What made the second set of instructions clear?

_____

You already have experience in giving instructions—explaining to someone how to reach a certain destination, for example, or how to perform a task. Your success in giving instructions is measured by whether or not your listener understands the instructions and performs the task.

▼ **Communication Tip**

Effective directions are:

☑ Clear

☑ Well organized

☑ Accurate

☑ Complete

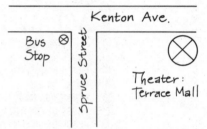

| Speaker Gives Instructions | → | Listener Understands the Instructions | → | Listener Performs the Task |

▼ Practice

A. Write directions explaining how to get to a certain destination—a neighborhood school, a local supermarket, a restaurant—from your home. Draw a map similar to the one on this page to accompany your oral directions.

B. Work with a partner. Tell your partner how to get to the destination you described in Part A. Your partner will listen and repeat the directions. Correct your partner if necessary.

Preparing Instructions

As you learned in Lesson 3, on-the-job speaking situations require you to think about what you want to say *before* you say it. The general strategies for effective speaking (see page 23) also apply to giving **oral directions**. Often, you will need to plan a set of instructions before you deliver the information orally to the listener. Explaining difficult tasks involves more planning than explaining simple tasks does. Here are the guidelines you should follow for preparing to give instructions.

Preparing Instructions

1. Identify the task you will teach.

2. Determine the listener's skill level and background knowledge.

3. Plan the instructions:

   - Write down who is to do the task and when it is to be done.

   - List all necessary equipment or materials.

   - Order the steps in the correct sequence.

   - Decide whether you will need to use a visual aid, such as a map or diagram. Also decide whether you will actually demonstrate the procedure.

   - Include precautions or warnings.

► When have you had to give oral directions? Did you write anything down first? Did you think first about what you had to say? Describe the situation.

_____

_____

_____

On the next two pages, you will read how Walter adapted these guidelines to explain the procedure for punching a time clock.

Making a Plan

Walter's boss told him to explain to Audrey, a new employee, the procedure for using the time clock. The boss mentioned that Audrey was only 17 and had never worked before.

Walter followed the guidelines you saw on page 49. First, he identified the task: using the time clock. Then he considered Audrey's background. Since she was quite young and had no work experience, Walter thought it might be helpful to give some background information about the time clock. He also knew he would need to give detailed information about the procedure.

Next, he planned his message. Here are his notes:

<u>Background info</u> : tell how company uses t.c. for payroll.

<u>Who/When</u> : all hourly employees / before and after work, before and after lunch.

<u>Equipment/Materials</u> : time clock, time card, rack

<u>Order of steps</u> :

1. Take card from rack

2. Insert in slot – name end first

3. When hear mechanical sound, remove card

4. Return card to rack

<u>Give demonstration</u>

<u>No precautions / warnings</u>

Walter reviewed his notes. An hour later, he met with Audrey to explain the procedure. On the next page, notice how Walter used his notes and applied effective speaking techniques in giving oral instructions.

Sending the Message

Read the dialogue below. (Two volunteers could read it aloud.)

Walter: Audrey, the boss asked me to tell you how to punch the time clock. Have you ever used one before?

Audrey: No, I haven't. I'm not familiar with them at all.

Walter: Well, there's really nothing to it. All employees working on an hourly rate punch the time clock. At the end of each week, the Payroll Department clerk collects the time cards. He multiplies the total hours stamped on the time card by your hourly rate.

Anyway, as you can see, our time clock is located right here inside the "Employees Only" entrance. The time cards are kept on this rack. They're arranged in alphabetical order, so it will be easy to find your card. Now this is important. You punch in when you get here in the morning, punch out before lunch, punch in after lunch, and punch out when you leave. With me so far?

Audrey: In other words, I punch the time clock before and after work and before and after lunch.

Walter: Exactly. Using the time clock is pretty simple. Here—I'll show you the procedure. The time clock has a slot in the middle. First, take your card from the rack, and insert the card into the slot. Make sure you insert the end with your name typed on it. When you hear a mechanical sound, remove your card from the slot. Then place your stamped card in the rack. Be sure the card is in correct alphabetical order. And that's it! Is there anything you'd like to ask?

Audrey: I understand the steps of the procedure, but would you watch me practice on a blank card?

Walter: Sure, go ahead.

▼ Practice

1. How does Walter's explanation show his understanding of the listener, Audrey? Give some examples.

2. How would you describe Walter's instructions? Give examples to support your answer.

3. Why is a demonstration helpful in teaching a task?

4. How does Audrey show that she understands *when* to use the time clock?

Constructing a Flow Chart

A flow chart is a diagram illustrating the sequence of steps in a procedure or process. You can make a simple flow chart by drawing boxes connected by arrows. For example, the flow chart below summarizes the main steps for punching a time clock.

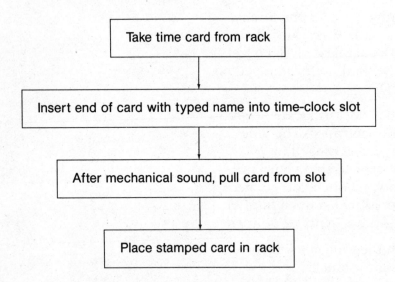

You probably noticed that the boxes represent the steps and the arrows represent the sequence of steps.

When you are giving oral instructions, constructing a flow chart benefits both you and the listener. A flow chart helps you visually organize the key steps you need to explain. After you have completed your explanation, you can use the flow chart as a handout for the listener. In turn, the listener has an easy-to-understand summary that he or she can use when actually performing your instructions.

▼ Practice

Think of a simple household chore consisting of several steps. Make a flow chart similar to the one above that explains how to perform the task. Write each step in the appropriate box.

Directions: This exercise will help you practice the guidelines for giving clear directions. Choose a partner to work with. Each of you will take turns playing the roles of a trainer and a trainee. Guidelines for both of these roles follow.

TRAINER'S GUIDELINES

Think of a task you frequently perform at your job or in your home—examples include operating a machine or an electrical appliance, preparing your favorite recipe, waxing the floor, or painting the walls. Then teach the task to your partner, the trainee. Fill out the Planning on the right below before you explain the instructions orally. (Use another sheet of paper if you need more space to write.)

Remember to maintain eye contact as you explain the instructions. Build two-way communication by inviting your partner to ask questions about the task.

TRAINEE'S GUIDELINES

Your role is to learn how to perform a specific task. Apply these techniques for listening to instructions:

1. Focus your attention.

2. Identify the task you are expected to perform.

3. Summon up your background knowledge.

4. Visualize the procedure.

5. Write down the steps.

6. Check your understanding.

7. If possible, actually perform the task or act it out.

PLANNING FORM:

GIVING ORAL INSTRUCTIONS

Task: how to _____

Technical or unfamiliar words to explain:

_____

When the task should be done: _____

_____

Necessary equipment or materials: _____

_____

Main steps in performing the task:

1. _____

2. _____

3. _____

4. _____

5. _____

Use visual aid? (If yes, explain.) _____

_____

Give demonstration? _____

Precautions or warnings: _____

_____

Safety First

Alice is a secretary at an advertising agency. She told Juanita, an office clerk, "I need 50 copies of this product description right away. The copy machine on this floor is out of order, so you'll have to use the one on the fifth floor. When you get off the elevator, make a sharp right turn. Go down to the end of the hallway. The copy machine is in the small room to your left.

"Now that machine jams sometimes. If it does, this is what you should do. First, turn off the machine. Slowly lift up the top of the machine as though you were lifting up the lid of a box. You'll probably see one or two sheets wrinkled between two rollers. Pull out the wrinkled sheets and lower the top of the copier until it snaps into place. Then all you have to do is turn the machine on again and press 'Start Print.' You shouldn't have any problems."

Juanita hurried to the fifth floor and began running off the copies. As Alice had predicted, the copy machine jammed in the middle of the job. Juanita followed Alice's instructions exactly. However, when Juanita pulled the wrinkled papers from the rollers, she burned her fingertips. Alice forgot to tell her not to touch the rollers because they were very hot. Fortunately, Juanita reacted quickly, so the burns were minor.

▼ **For Discussion**

1. Are Alice's instructions clear? accurate? well organized? complete?

2. Have you ever received incomplete instructions? What happened?

3. What are the safety hazards of operating an electrical appliance or tool you often use?

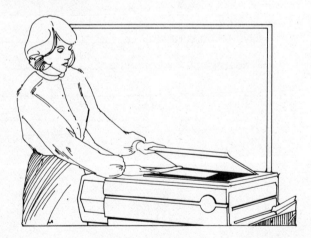

ON YOUR OWN

Construct a flow chart illustrating how to remove paper from a jammed copy machine. Use the story above as your source of information.

Receiving Telephone Calls

The Davis family is relaxing in the living room when the telephone rings.

Phone Operator: I have a collect call from Carla Davis.

Jennifer: I'll accept the charges.

Phone Operator: Please hold. I will connect you with the other party.

(Jennifer yells to her children in the living room, "Turn off the TV. I'm talking to Aunt Carla long distance.")

Carla: Hello, Jennifer. I'm glad I caught you. I'm calling from the St. Louis airport. My flight to Chicago was canceled because of the heavy fog.

Jennifer: Good timing—I was just going to call the airport to find out if your plane was on schedule.

Carla: I've made arrangements for another flight, so I'll be arriving later tonight. Can you still pick me up?

Jennifer: Sure, no problem. Let me write down the information.

Carla: I'll be flying on Worldwide Airlines. The flight number is 321. The

Often, travelers need to make phone calls.

plane is scheduled to arrive at 10:15 P.M.

Jennifer: *(reading back her notes)* Worldwide Flight 321, arriving at 10:15.

Carla: That's right. See you tonight.

Jennifer: We're all looking forward to your visit. Bye, Carla.

Talk About It

- During her phone conversation, how does Jennifer screen out distractions? take brief notes?
- How does she make sure that she understands Carla's message?
- Think of a time when you took an important phone message at home. How did you check the accuracy of your message?

Phone Calls in Everyday Life

When you receive phone calls at work, your telephone manner and speech may vary from caller to caller. For example, when you receive calls at home from close friends or relatives, your conversations are casual. When you receive business calls at home, you are probably more formal and think about what you say more carefully.

Notice how Nancy Sims responds to different callers—Barbara Dawson, her best friend, and Clarice Watts, a customer-service representative. (Two volunteers could read the following dialogues aloud to the class.)

Personal Call

Nancy: Hello.

Barbara: Hi, Nancy. What's new?

Nancy: Same old thing. Oh, yeah, I forgot to tell you. We're getting cable TV. The kids are all excited.

Barbara: That's great. Bob and I love the movies on cable.

Nancy: Yeah, that's the main reason we got it. So what's going on with you?

Barbara: I was thinking about dropping by later today.

Nancy: Sure, any time.

Barbara: OK, I'll see you in a few hours. Bye.

Nancy: See ya. Bye.

Business Call

Nancy: Hello.

Clarice: Hello, is this Nancy Sims?

Nancy: Yes, who's calling, please?

Clarice: This is Clarice Watts from Cable TV Enterprises. I'm calling to let you know that our technicians will be at your house about nine o'clock tomorrow morning. They're going to install the cable wire and put a converter on the TV. Is this a convenient time?

Nancy: Yes, I'll be home.

Clarice: Good. I hope you enjoy your cable TV.

Nancy: I'm sure I will. Thank you for calling. Good-bye.

Clarice: Good-bye.

▼ Practice

1. What is the difference between how Nancy greets the caller and says good-bye in each conversation?

2. What casual words does Nancy use in her personal call?

3. Does Nancy use any of these casual words in her business call?

On the Job

Receiving business calls at work is similar to receiving business calls at home: the language you use will be more formal and polite than the language you use for personal calls. Also, since the caller can't see you, you have to rely entirely on your voice to show your interest in the caller and to convey information.

How do you sound when you are talking on the phone? Take a moment to evaluate your speech habits.

- Does your tone of voice express a courteous, helpful attitude?

- Do you pronounce words clearly?

- Do you speak too slowly or too rapidly?

- Do you speak too loudly or too softly?

You represent your workplace whenever you use the phone for business purposes. Your telephone personality—a pleasant tone of voice and clear speech—will create a favorable impression of your workplace and its employees.

Receiving Business Calls

Most workplaces expect employees to follow a formal procedure for answering the phone. At your job, practice the guidelines listed below.

Receiving Calls: Guidelines

1. **Answer the phone promptly.** If possible, pick up the phone on the first ring.

2. **Identify yourself immediately.** Tell the caller the name of your workplace (or your department) and your name. For example, "Hello, Shipping Department, Daniel Chin."

3. **Make the caller feel welcome.** Be considerate. Provide the help or information the caller needs.

4. **Listen carefully and be prepared to take notes.** Give the caller your full attention. If necessary, write down important information.

5. **Use polite language and a pleasant tone of voice.**

The dialogues on the next two pages illustrate the wrong way and the right way to receive phone calls in a business setting.

Receiving a Business Call: Version 1

Read the following telephone dialogue. Two volunteers could read the dialogue aloud.

Ms. Smith: Yes?

Ms. Gámez: Is this Jefferson Health Clinic?

Ms. Smith: (*speaking fast*) Yeah. What do you need?

Ms. Gámez: Well, I was calling to find out my test results. I came in Monday for a—

Ms. Smith: (*interrupting*) What is your name?

Ms. Gámez: It's Laura Gámez. That's G-a-m-e-z.

Ms. Smith: (*after a pause*) I'm sorry. We don't have records for anyone named Laura Gómez.

Ms. Gámez: My name isn't Gómez, it's *Gámez.* G-a-m-e-z.

Ms. Smith: Oh, why didn't you say so? Here it is. Now, what was it you wanted?

Ms. Gámez: My test results. Dr. Banerji told me to call for them today.

Ms. Smith: Was it a CBC?

Ms. Gámez: What's a CBC?

Ms. Smith: (*sighing loudly*) A complete blood count! Was that the test you had?

Ms. Gámez: Well, it was a blood test to see if I have anemia.

Ms. Smith: Anyway, it doesn't matter. I see the results aren't in anyway.

Ms. Gámez: Oh. Well, when would I be able to get them?

Ms. Smith: I really couldn't tell you.

Ms. Gámez: All right. I guess I'll try again tomorrow.

▼ Practice

1. Does Ms. Smith show courtesy toward Ms. Gámez? Give examples to explain your answer.

2. Is Ms. Smith an effective listener?

3. Why does Ms. Gámez have trouble understanding Ms. Smith's information?

Receiving a Business Call: Version 2

Read the following telephone dialogue. Two volunteers could read the dialogue aloud.

Ms. Smith: Jefferson Health Clinic, Lynn Smith.

Ms. Gámez: Hello. I'm calling to find out some test results. I came in on Monday to be tested for anemia.

Ms. Smith: I'll be happy to check. Your name, please?

Ms. Gámez: Laura Gámez. That's G-a-m-e-z.

Ms. Smith: Could you hold, Ms. Gámez, while I check?

Ms. Gámez: Sure.

Ms. Smith: I see you had a complete blood count, but the results aren't in yet, I'm afraid. They should be ready tomorrow.

Ms. Gámez: That's strange. Dr. Banerji told me they'd be available today.

Ms. Smith: Sometimes the lab takes an extra day on these tests. Why don't you try at about ten o'clock tomorrow morning?

Ms. Gámez: OK, I will. Thank you.

Ms. Smith: You're welcome. Good-bye.

▼ Practice

1. Is Ms. Smith polite during her phone conversation with Ms. Gámez? Give examples to explain your answer.

2. Does Ms. Smith follow the proper guidelines for answering the phone at work?

3. Why is this conversation so short?

Receiving Business Calls: DO's and DON'Ts

- **DO** use courteous expressions such as "please" and "thank you."

- **DO** identify yourself when you answer.

- **DO** give clear and accurate information.

- **DON'T** act unfriendly or impatient.

- **DON'T** rudely interrupt callers.

- **DON'T** use technical words that callers may not understand.

Taking Messages

Terry is an office clerk in the sales department of a printing company. One morning Richard, a sales representative, told Terry, "I'm going to a meeting. Could you please take my telephone calls? You can write down the messages on the forms next to my phone. Thanks."

Fifteen minutes later, Richard's phone rang.

Terry: Sales Department, Richard McClain's office, Terry speaking.

Roy: Hello, this is Roy Loesch at Atlas Advertising Agency. Is Mr. McClain available?

Terry: I'm sorry, but Mr. McClain is away from his office right now. May I take a message?

Roy: Yes. Tell him I have a rush order for a printing job. Have him call me back as soon as possible. My phone number is 555-3541, extension 431.

Terry: That's 555-3541, extension 431.

Roy: Correct.

Terry: Mr. Loesch, would you please spell your last name?

Roy: L-o-e-s-c-h.

Terry: I'll give him the message.

Roy: Thank you. Good-bye.

Terry: You're welcome. Good-bye.

As Roy was speaking, Terry wrote his name and phone number on a message form. He left the form on Richard's desk.

At your job, your coworkers may ask you to answer their phones when they are away from their offices or work areas. Like Terry, you should immediately state your department, your coworker's name, and your name. If a message form is not available, jot down the following information:

- caller's name, company, and phone number
- time and date of the call
- caller's message

To practice filling out a telephone message form, see page 91.

Directions: This activity will help you apply the guidelines for receiving phone calls to a real-life situation. Work with a partner. Each of you will take turns playing the roles of a telephone caller and an order taker. To make the exchange more like a real phone call, turn your chairs away so you cannot see each other. Guidelines for each of the roles follow.

TELEPHONE CALLER'S GUIDELINES

Imagine you are calling Dante's Pizza Parlor. You want to order a pizza for delivery.

THIN-CRUST PIZZA			
	Small (12")	Medium (14")	Large (16")
Cheese	$5.00	$6.25	$7.50
Each extra ingredient*	$1.00	$1.25	$1.50
*sausage, pepperoni, mushrooms, green peppers, onions, garlic, black olives			

1. Select from the menu below the pizza you would like to order. Include the size and the ingredients.

2. Tell the telephone order taker your selection. Give your partner any additional information that he or she may request.

TELEPHONE ORDER TAKER'S GUIDELINES

Imagine you are an order taker at Dante's Pizza Parlor. Your telephone manner should reflect the pizza parlor's reputation for fast, friendly service.

1. Answer the phone. State the pizza parlor's name and your name. Ask the caller what he or she would like to order.

2. Listen carefully. Jot down the order on the delivery receipt below. Also, find out the caller's name, address, and telephone number. Include this information on the order form.

3. Check for accuracy by restating the caller's pizza order and address.

4. Tell the caller the pizza will be delivered in an hour, and thank your partner for calling Dante's Pizza Parlor.

Delivery Receipt

Customer's Name _____

Deliver to _____

Date _____   Phone _____

_____

Order   Price

The Angry Caller

Kirk: Hi-Tech Appliances, Kirk Holmes.

Roger: (*angrily*) This is Roger Jackson. A refrigerator was scheduled to be delivered to my home this afternoon. It's four thirty and the refrigerator hasn't arrived. What's the problem?

Kirk: May I have your name and address?

Roger: I already told you my name. It's Roger Jackson. I live at 367 West Kenton, Bradleyville.

Kirk: Mr. Jackson, please wait while I check the delivery schedule.

Roger: I've been waiting all afternoon. Make it fast.

Kirk: I'm sorry, Mr. Jackson, you apparently have mixed up the dates. The refrigerator is scheduled to be delivered tomorrow.

Roger: No, you mixed up the dates! Some idiot at your store told me that today was the delivery date. I can't afford to take another afternoon off work.

Kirk: (*loses his temper*) Don't dump your problems on me, Mr. Jackson. It's not my fault you got the days of the week confused. You'll get your refrigerator tomorrow. (*hangs up the phone*)

Bad Telephone Manners

Marilyn: (*after 10 rings*) Hello.

Debbie: (*confused*) Is this Lakeside Medical Center?

Marilyn: (*chewing gum*) Yeah.

Debbie: May I speak to Lucille Weaver? I'm supposed to contact her about my payment notice.

Marilyn: She's on a coffee break or something. I don't know where she is. Call back later. (*hangs up*)

▼ **For Discussion**

1. Did Kirk handle the angry caller effectively?

2. What may happen as a result of this phone call?

3. Explain why you *agree* or *disagree* with each of the following statements.

   a. Don't directly tell callers they are wrong.

   b. Maintain self-control when you talk to an angry customer on the phone.

   c. Don't take an angry caller's remarks personally.

▼ **For Discussion**

1. Did Marilyn follow the correct procedure for receiving a business call? Give reasons to explain your answer.

2. What advice would you give Marilyn about receiving a business call?

Initiating Telephone Calls

Roberta's son hurt himself while playing with a new toy airplane. Roberta had heard about a hotline number people could call to report unsafe products. She turned to the page entitled "Hotline Numbers" in her phone book and read these tips for calling hotlines:

1. Think about what you want before you call. Be as specific as possible.
2. Call early in the day before the source becomes bogged down. Most people are in their offices and ready to work in the morning.
3. Encourage your source at the hotline to give you further information or referrals to other sources.
4. Be sure to get the name, address, and telephone number of any source you are referred to.
5. Be polite and appreciative.

Early the next morning, Roberta called the hotline.

Operator: Consumer Safety Hotline.

Roberta: Hello. My name is Roberta Dawson. I would like to report an unsafe toy.

Hotline workers receive dozens of calls every day.

Operator: (*taking notes*) Ms. Dawson, could you please tell me the name of the toy and the manufacturer?

Roberta: The toy is a metal airplane called "Super Jet," manufactured by Kids Only in Boston, Massachusetts.

Operator: Please describe your complaint.

Roberta: Well, the metal blades on the propellers cut my son's fingers. Also, the metal airplane wings are very sharp and could injure children.

Operator: I see. We'll follow up on your complaint as soon as possible.

Roberta: Thank you for your help.

Talk About It

- Did Roberta follow the tips for calling hotlines?
- Why is politeness more effective than anger for reporting complaints?
- Have you ever complained about a product? What happened?

Personal and Business Calls

When you call close friends and relatives, you probably don't have to identify yourself. You assume they recognize your voice. Your conversations may be aimless when you are calling just to say hello. You may use informal expressions, such as "yeah," "nope," or "hey, can you hang on?"

In contrast, when you initiate, or make, business calls from your home, your telephone manner is probably more formal and your conversations more organized.

▶ What personal business calls have you made lately?

Typical examples include reserving airplane tickets, arranging medical appointments, and ordering carry-out food. In these situations, you would plan the call beforehand. You might also need to write brief notes.

Notice the different approaches Kim Hogan uses in calling two people—her brother Keith and a store clerk. (Two volunteers could read aloud the following dialogues.)

Personal Call

Keith: Hello.

Kim: Hi, Keith. How are you?

Keith: Hi, Kim! I'm just fine. What's up?

Kim: Are you doing anything Friday night?

Keith: No, I haven't made any plans yet.

Kim: Why don't you come over and watch a video?

Keith: Sure.

Kim: We were thinking of renting *Sea of Love*, starring Al Pacino.

Keith: Oh, yeah, he plays a cop. That's a good choice. I never saw it.

Kim: OK, then we'll see you Friday around 7 o'clock. Bye, Keith.

Keith: Bye, Kim.

Business Call

Clerk: Hollywood Video Showplace, Brian Anderson. May I help you?

Kim: Yes, this is Kimberly Hogan. I'm a member of your video rental club. I'd like to reserve a movie for this Friday, the 15th.

Clerk: What movie would you like to rent?

Kim: *Sea of Love.*

Clerk: Let's see . . . it's available. Do you have your membership card handy?

Kim: Yes.

Clerk: Please read your ID number slowly as I call it up on the computer.

Kim: 2-9-8-3-1.

Clerk: Everything is arranged, Ms. Hogan. Please pick up your video before 5 P.M.

Kim: Thank you. Good-bye.

Clerk: You're welcome. Good-bye.

Making Calls at Work

Besides receiving calls at your job, you will also initiate calls. In both of these situations, you will need these skills.

CALLER

RECEIVER

- Active listening
- Clear speaking habits
- Courteous attitude
- Pleasant tone of voice

Remember, you represent your workplace whenever you use the phone for business purposes. How can you convey a positive image of your workplace? What procedures should you follow for placing business calls? To initiate business calls effectively, practice the guidelines listed below.

Initiating Calls: Guidelines

1. **Plan the call in advance.** Jot down your purpose for calling and, if necessary, the questions you want answered. Gather all the materials you need—a credit card, business forms, and so on.

2. **Check the number before calling.** Make sure you're dialing the correct number.

3. **Allow time for the person to answer.** You should let the phone ring about 10 times before hanging up.

4. **Identify yourself immediately.** Give your full name and the workplace's name.

5. **Be prepared to take notes.** Keep a pen and paper handy so you can write down important information or answers to your questions.

The dialogues on the next two pages illustrate the wrong way and the right way of making a phone call in a business setting.

Initiating a Business Call: Version 1

Two volunteers should read aloud the following dialogue.

Anna: Hello, Metro Office Supplies, Anna Wong. May I help you?

Jake: Yeah. Did you receive my order for the computer paper yet?

Anna: Who's calling, please?

Jake: Oh, right. This is Jake DeWitt. I'm an office assistant at R&W Insurance. Anyway, did you get my order for computer paper or not? I mailed it a couple of days ago. You should have it by now.

Anna: Mr. DeWitt, may I have your company's account number and the purchase order number?

Jake: (*rummaging through the papers on his desk*) I just saw the purchase order on my desk a minute ago. Hang on. I'll check my files. (*one minute later*) Nope, can't find it. Anyway, the guy who takes the inventory of the supply room messed up. He told me we were running low on computer paper. Later he finds a dozen boxes of computer paper stacked in a corner. So, of course, we don't need it anymore. That's the reason I'm calling. Just cancel the order.

Anna: I'd like to help you, Mr. DeWitt, but we follow a certain procedure for canceling orders. I need your company's account number, the purchase order number, and the exact description of your order. Could you please call me back with this information?

Jake: (*annoyed*) OK, OK. I'll call you back. I don't know what the big deal is. All I want to do is cancel the order. Good-bye.

▼ Practice

1. Who is responsible—Anna or Jake—for the communication problems that occurred during the phone conversation? Why?

2. Did Jake plan his phone call in advance? Give reasons to explain your answer.

3. Should Jake have told Anna about the inventory clerk's mistake? Give reasons to explain your answer.

Initiating a Business Call: Version 2

Two volunteers should read aloud the following dialogue.

Anna: Hello, Metro Office Supplies, Anna Wong. May I help you?

Jake: Yes, this is Jake DeWitt from R&W Insurance Company. I mailed a purchase order for computer paper two days ago. Have you received the order?

Anna: I'll check, Mr. DeWitt. May I have your company's account number and the purchase order number?

Jake: (*speaking more slowly*) The account number is 9-0-8-4-2. The purchase order number is 0-0-4-1.

Anna: We received your purchase order this morning. Would you like to make an adjustment?

Jake: Yes, I would like to cancel the order for one dozen boxes of ComputerRite paper. I just discovered that we already have a sufficient supply.

Anna: I appreciate your notifying me so promptly, Mr. DeWitt. I'll process the cancellation right away.

Jake: Thank you for your help. Good-bye.

Anna: You're welcome. Good-bye.

▼ Practice

1. Did Jake efficiently use the time he spent talking to Anna? Give reasons to explain your answer.

2. How would you describe Jake's manner on the phone?

3. Do you think Anna has a favorable impression of R&W Insurance, Jack's employer? Why or why not?

Initiating Business Calls: DO's and DON'Ts

- DO prepare for your phone calls.
- DO identify yourself and your workplace immediately.
- DO clearly state your reason for calling.
- DO discuss only important information.
- DO show respect for the other person.

- DON'T waste the other person's time.
- DON'T discuss details unrelated to the business call.
- DON'T give the person the impression that you're disorganized.
- DON'T act overly demanding.

An Important Reminder

In Lesson 3, you thought about how to separate your private life from your working life. The calls you place at work should be related to business unless you have a personal emergency. However, some employees assume that they can also use the phone to place personal calls. For example, Jason, an office worker, frequently calls his friends whenever he becomes bored with his work.

▶ What effects does making personal calls have on a business?

_____

Some possible effects are listed below.

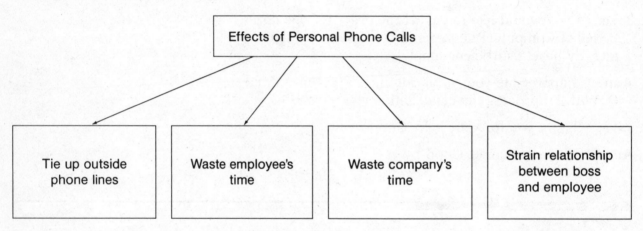

Therefore, *limit* your personal phone calls while you're at work.

▼ Practice

Read the situation described below. Then discuss the questions that follow.

> Donna is a clerical assistant at a small business in Florida. She is in the process of getting a divorce and is letting her home life interfere with her work. When she arrives at work, she closes her office door and uses the phone to resolve her personal problems. Donna calls her lawyer to discuss her divorce settlement. She also calls her friends to talk about her husband. As a result, she does not complete her work on time.

1. If you were Donna's boss, how would you handle this situation?

2. What effect could Donna's behavior have on her coworkers?

Directions: This activity will help you apply the guidelines for initiating phone calls to a real-life situation. Choose a partner to work with. Each of you will take turns playing the roles of a telephone caller and a receiver of a telephone call. To make the phone conversation more realistic, turn your chairs so you cannot see each other. Guidelines for each of the roles follow.

CALLER'S GUIDELINES

Imagine you're interested in buying merchandise advertised in the classified section of the newspaper. Choose one of the ads below, or cut out an ad from the newspaper. Show the ad to your partner.

You will pretend to call the person listed in the ad because you want more information about the items he or she is selling. After you have selected an ad, follow this procedure:

1. Jot down specific questions you would like to ask about the items. Use the words *who, what, when, where, why,* and *how* to help formulate your questions.

2. Identify yourself and your reason for calling.

3. Get additional information about the item for sale. Refer to your written questions.

4. Arrange an appointment to see the item. Ask for the address.

5. End the call courteously.

RECEIVER'S GUIDELINES

Carefully read the ad your partner has chosen. Imagine you are the person who placed this ad in the newspaper.

1. Pretend you are answering the phone.

2. Answer the caller's questions as well as you can. Use your imagination to make the item you're selling sound real and appealing.

3. Settle on a time and date when your partner can see the item.

4. Ask your partner for his or her phone number and write it down.

5. End the call courteously.

MACHINIST TOOLS WITH BOX PLUS SOME PLUMBING TOOLS Jack 708-555-5894	POOL TABLE, GOOD CONDITION $300, LINCOLN PARK LOCATION Mike, 312-555-3987

MOVING SALE: 1 black lacquer dining room set, 6-piece setting. Must sell. Beth 414-555-8700	25-inch color TV, beautiful picture, good sound, $120 Call Pat, 312-555-0980

COCKER SPANIEL PUPPIES Dale 414-555-5967	CAT: Orange Tabby, Male To good home 708-555-3845

The Disorganized Caller

Jay: Good morning, Product Services Department, Jay Landford.

Brent: (*excited*) Our photocopier is broken. The images come out blurry, and there are dark streaks down the page. We just bought the machine, so I really don't understand why we should be having a problem with it.

Jay: Excuse me, sir, but who is this?

Brent: Oh, yeah, I forgot to tell you. This is Brent Johnson. We need the photocopier repaired right away.

Jay: Mr. Johnson, I need to know the name of your company.

Brent: Oh, yeah. Shannon, Lawrence, and Associates. We're a small law office handling mostly personal injury cases. I'm an office clerk here, which means I get stuck doing the photocopying. I've got tons of letters and briefs to run off by the end of the day. If the photocopier doesn't get fixed, I know Mr. Shannon is going to throw a fit.

Jay: (*trying to remain patient*) Mr. Johnson, does your law office have an account with us?

Brent: Sure, long before I started working here. Rosie Sanchez usually requests the repairs. She's on vacation, so Mr. Shannon told me to give you a ring.

Jay: As we were speaking, I looked up your account. Your law office is located at 421 Willow Drive, and your phone number is 555-0021. Correct?

Brent: You got it right.

Jay: Well, Mr. Johnson, I'm sorry your office has been experiencing problems with the new photocopier. I'll try to schedule a repairperson for early this afternoon. I'll call you right back.

Brent: (*hanging up*) The sooner, the better.

▼ For Discussion

1. What advice would you give Brent about making business phone calls?

2. What unimportant information did Brent include in his phone conversation?

3. How did Jay effectively handle this difficult phone call?

4. Why do disorganized phone calls waste time?

Attending Meetings

The Hotspot, a dance club, was located directly behind a six-unit apartment building. The Hotspot blasted loud music nightly from 9 P.M. to 2 A.M.

Several building residents complained to the club's owner, but the music continued to blare each night. Finally, the residents decided to have a meeting about the problem.

The residents gathered in the apartment of Calvin, who chaired the meeting. "Good evening," he said. "We've come together tonight to decide what we can do as a group to stop the noise from the Hotspot. By the end of the meeting, let's see if we can have a list of possible actions to take."

"How about contacting our city councilman?" suggested Kendra. "He helped to close that bar a few years ago where all those rowdy people were messing up the neighborhood. And he's always had a good record for listening to the people in the ward. Look at all the community meetings he sponsors."

"Oh, politicians!" scoffed Gordon. "You can trust 'em about as far as you can throw 'em. Forget the councilman. Forget the mayor. Forget the senators."

"Well, what do you suggest we do, Gordon?" asked Diana.

"I don't know. Don't ask me! But I'm not going to any politician. No sir."

Gordon continued for another five minutes until Calvin got a word in edgewise. "Let's get some more suggestions on the table," he proposed.

An hour and a half later, the group had a list of possible actions to take:

- Contact the councilman, explain the situation, and ask for his support

- Write a group-complaint letter to the Hotspot's owner

- Consult a lawyer about our legal rights

Talk About It

- Did the meeting accomplish its purpose?
- What problem occurred in the meeting?
- Have you ever attended a community meeting? What was it like?

Group Decision Making

Meetings may be called simply to share information, but more often they involve **decision making**, such as planning or problem solving.

At times, attending a meeting can be a frustrating experience. When the people have no clear idea of what is to be discussed or decided, the meeting will be confused and unfocused. When a person rambles on without making a point, or when someone states opinions without supporting them, others at the meeting will feel their time is being wasted. When everyone is busy stating opinions but ignoring anyone else's views, no decisions can be arrived at. An ineffective meeting can drag on for hours and end with no action taken.

Attending an effective meeting, on the other hand, can actually be a satisfying experience. People leave the meeting with a new understanding of a situation. They feel a sense of accomplishment because decisions were made. In addition, they often feel better able to work closely with others. They may have gained insights into other people's concerns, and their roles may be more clearly defined.

Here are some general guidelines for effective group decision making.

Guidelines for Group Decision Making

1. **Know the purpose of the meeting.** Whenever possible, find out in advance what is to be discussed or decided.

2. **Be prepared for the meeting.** Before the meeting, gather together your own thoughts and ideas on the decisions to be made.

3. **Support your opinions.** Give reasons or evidence for your views.

4. **Be open to other points of view.** Listen carefully to opinions that differ from your own.

5. **Avoid arguing with each other.** When the group continues to disagree on a point, try to reach a compromise.

▶ Have you ever attended a meeting that was frustrating? How could it have been more successful?

Meet with four classmates. Imagine you are among a crew of five flying a cargo plane full of supplies to a scientific research station in the Arctic. Your plane malfunctions and crash-lands 100 miles from the research station.

Fortunately, all five crew members survive, but three of you receive leg injuries and cannot walk far. The remaining two must walk the 100 miles over open ice and snow to get help.

A number of items survive the crash. The crew members set aside enough provisions and equipment for the injured, who will stay behind. Once this has been done, there are 20 items left. However, the two walking crew members can carry a total of only 10 items.

Your group has two tasks:

1. Decide which 10 items the two crew members should carry.

2. Rank these 10 items in importance, with 1 as the most important item and 10 as the least important. Some items may have to be left behind along the way, so your group should decide which items are most vital.

3. Choose 5 items that the injured crew members need to keep with them until help arrives.

pillows	pickax
down sleeping bags	shovel
tent	kerosene cooking stove
flares	kerosene
box of matches	rifle
hunting knife	portable heater*
toilet paper	portable radio*
flashlight*	binoculars
packets of dehydrated food	compass
bottled water	first-aid kit

*batteries are included

Use the group decision-making guidelines from page 72.

Critical Listening

When you attend a meeting, you will need to develop your skills in **critical listening**. Critical listening enables you to distinguish **facts** from **opinions**.

Suppose you are a member of the Parents' Council of your local high school. You are serving on a committee to discuss a billboard located across the street from the school. The president of the Parents' Council begins the meeting with the following statement. Read the statement silently, or a volunteer may read it aloud to the class.

Teenage alcoholism is a serious problem in our community. As you have already noticed, the billboard across the street advertises whiskey. An attractive young man and woman are clinking shot glasses. The advertising slogan reads, "Lightning Whiskey. It's So Smooth." I think we should send a letter demanding that the liquor

company remove the billboard. High school students who see the sign everyday will imitate the young couple and start drinking whiskey.

▶ Label each of the president's statements below as a fact or an opinion.

_____ **1.** The billboard across the street advertises whiskey.

_____ **2.** High school students who see the sign everyday will imitate the young couple and start drinking whiskey.

The president's first statement is a fact because it can be proven true: anyone can look outside and see the billboard standing there. The second statement, however, is an opinion—the president's personal prediction of the billboard's effects on teenagers. As a council member, you might agree or disagree with the president's opinion.

You should listen critically whenever people at a meeting try to persuade you to agree with their viewpoints. You should determine whether or not their facts support the opinions they express. You will then be better equipped to judge the value of their ideas and statements.

Staff Meetings

At your job, you will attend meetings in which you participate in group discussions. For example, your boss will probably schedule staff meetings to assign tasks, explain new procedures, and solve problems.

In addition to participating in staff meetings, you may also have the opportunity to serve on committees. For instance, as a member of the social committee, you might plan company-sponsored activities—picnics, softball teams, holiday parties, and so on.

When you are invited to join a group discussion at work, what are your responsibilities as an active participant? Listed below are some guidelines to follow for staff meetings.

Participating at Staff Meetings: Guidelines

- **Prepare for the meeting.** Whenever possible, find out in advance the topic or topics of the discussion. Study any written information you receive about the meeting. Jot down your opinions about the topic and support them with facts.

- **Arrive on time.** Latecomers to meetings often disrupt the ongoing discussion.

- **Follow the discussion attentively.** Listen carefully and take notes on key points. Consider new ideas with an open mind. Don't tune out a speaker whose viewpoint differs from yours.

- **Show courtesy to other group members.** Don't interrupt other participants when they are speaking. Avoid carrying on disruptive conversations with the person seated next to you. Most important, show interest in what others are saying.

- **Express your comments clearly and concisely.** Think about what you want to say *before* you speak. Make your point quickly, and don't ramble on with needless information.

- **Know what is expected of you at the end of the meeting.** When the meeting is over, you should know whether you are expected to take any action, such as performing a new task or finding out information to present at the next meeting. Be sure to find out if and when another meeting has been scheduled.

Effective Group Behavior

Meetings usually run smoothly if everyone is prepared and respectfully exchanges ideas and information. Unfortunately, many meetings are not effective. One person talks too much, while another remains silent. Some members, more eager to speak than to listen, interrupt other people. One participant disagrees with someone else's opinion, so he harshly criticizes it. Another individual raises issues unrelated to the topic discussed at the meeting. These communication problems may cause conflict and waste time.

▼ Practice

Work in groups of three people. Listed below are statements people have made at business meetings. One volunteer in your group should read each statement aloud. Then work together to identify the statements that are positive responses to communication problems. Place a check mark next to each positive statement.

1. "That's a lousy idea. It will never work." ☐

2. "You're wrong. Let me straighten you out about a few things." ☐

3. "Let's hear from some other group members. We can all benefit from listening to a variety of opinions." ☐

4. "That's enough already. Why don't you give someone else a chance to talk? You're not the only person with something to say." ☐

5. "I respect your opinion, but I have a different viewpoint." ☐

6. "Can't you stick to the topic? We don't have time to get sidetracked with unrelated issues." ☐

7. "You haven't said one word. Don't you have anything worthwhile to say?" ☐

8. "We haven't heard from you yet. Given your experience, would you like to offer some comments?" ☐

9. "Stop interrupting me! I haven't finished my point." ☐

10. "Excuse me. Could I please finish making my point here?" ☐

Directions: This activity will help you practice the discussion skills you have learned in this chapter. Meet in groups of six people. Pretend each of you is serving on a committee to discuss the cigarette-smoking policy at your job. Two of the committee members should play the roles of smokers, and four should play the roles of nonsmokers. Before you meet, carefully read the written statement you all received from your boss.

COMMITTEE MEETING: OFFICE SMOKING POLICY

Several employees in our office have requested that we establish a smoking policy. Nonsmokers are complaining that the cigarette smoke in the office is endangering their health. Some suggestions for resolving this situation are listed below:

- Ban smoking entirely.
- Divide the office equally into smoking and nonsmoking areas.
- Install clean-air filters to remove the smoke.
- Offer company-sponsored "stop-smoking" clinics.

I would like your committee to discuss and evaluate these suggestions and to add some of your own. After your meeting, please summarize in writing the main points of your discussion.

COMMITTEE MEMBERS' GUIDELINES:
Discussion Techniques

1. Before beginning the meeting, carefully read and think about the statement from the boss. Think of reasons that support your opinions and write them down.

2. Take notes during the discussion.

3. Discuss each suggestion in the order it appears on the written statement.

4. Defend your opinion with facts or reasons.

5. Keep an open mind. Listen carefully to opposing viewpoints. Withhold personal judgments until the person has finished speaking.

6. Keep your comments brief. Don't dominate the discussion or stray from the topic.

7. Avoid arguing. Remember, each suggestion does not have to meet everyone's approval.

8. At the end of the meeting, one member, with the help of the others, should write up a brief summary of the meeting's outcome. Another member should be prepared to present this information to the rest of the class.

Signs are frequently used to indicate Smoking and No Smoking areas.

The Ineffective Meeting

Lucy is the manager of a real estate office. She has called a staff meeting with five clerical assistants—Chris, Martin, Ellen, Ken, and Gina.

Lucy: Sorry, but I didn't have time to send you a memo detailing the purpose of this meeting. Anyway, I want to discuss the pros and cons of instituting flextime here.

Chris, Gina, and Martin: (*speaking at the same time*) What's flextime?

Lucy: Oh, I figured you already knew about it. Right now all our employees work from 9 to 5. With flextime, you can choose the eight-hour schedule you'd like to work.

Ken: You mean I can work from noon to 8. That would be great.

Lucy: (*speaking too quickly*) No. Your options are 7 to 3, 8 to 4, 9 to 5, or 10 to 6.

Gina: I'm going to choose 7 to 3. I'm up early with the kids anyway. If I leave at 3, I'll be there when the kids get home from school, and . . .

Lucy: Excuse me, but the purpose of this meeting is to discuss the advantages and disadvantages of flextime. You don't have to choose your option today.

Gina: Like I was saying, it's an advantage for me because I'm up at 5 A.M. anyway. And I feel guilty when the kids come home to an empty house.

Lucy: Thank you, Gina, but you've already made that point. Does anyone else have an opinion?

Martin: Sounds OK to me. I like it.

Ken: I think we should keep things the way they are.

Chris: So do I. I think flextime might cause some confusion in the office. We'll have to reorganize the deadlines for our work because everyone will be on a different schedule.

Lucy: That's a good point. Ellen, what is your opinion of flextime?

Ellen: It doesn't make any difference. I still have to work eight hours.

▼ For Discussion

1. What information should Lucy have given the clerical assistants before the meeting?

2. How well did Lucy handle the discussion? Did she make positive comments to help deal with communication problems?

3. Review the purpose of the meeting. At the meeting, whose comments truly related to the purpose? Explain.

4. What advice would you give Gina about participating at a meeting?

Performance Evaluations

Sports Break: An Interview with a Pro Football Coach

Reporter: Coach, now that the football season is over, how would you rate Curtis's performance as a quarterback?

Coach: Curtis often makes outstanding contributions to the team, but he's inconsistent. One game he's effective and throws for a lot of touchdowns. The next game he seems to lose his concentration, throws interceptions, and makes mistakes.

He doesn't always respond well to pressure, especially when the team is losing. Curtis and I have discussed ways he can develop his leadership ability— how he can better motivate the players to win the game. He's a young player and is trying to build his self-confidence. He has a promising career ahead of him. But he does need to work on some problems off the field.

Reporter: Could you give me an example?

Coach: Well, this is strictly off the record, but you know, Curtis loves being interviewed by the press. And, quite frankly, I think he talks too much. He publicly criticizes his teammates. For instance, Curtis told a reporter that Mark Hunter, a rookie, looks like a teenager playing touch football in the schoolyard. I've told Curtis that remarks like these damage team morale. Evaluating other players on the team is my job, not his.

Reporter: Coach, what method do you use for evaluating players' performances?

Coach: The day after the game, I meet with the team and the assistant coaches. We all watch a videotape of the game and review key plays. Based on our observations, the assistant coaches and I either praise or criticize certain players' performances in particular situations. We also discuss total team effort.

Talk About It

- How does the coach evaluate players?
- According to the coach, what are Curtis's strengths? What are his weaknesses?
- Curtis publicly criticized his teammate during a TV pres conference. At a job, what happens when employees openly criticize their coworkers?
- At a job, why are teamwork and morale important?

Learning from Evaluations

How can you learn to become more effective in doing your job? How can you increase your chances of getting a raise or a promotion? One way of achieving both of these goals is to benefit from your boss's **evaluation** of your job performance.

While you are performing your job, your boss observes your progress. For instance, Vanessa is a cashier at a drugstore. When she first started working there, she sometimes made mistakes ringing up items. She was trying to work too quickly. Bruce, Vanessa's manager, told her, "Slow down, Vanessa. When you're operating the cash register, concentrate on accuracy." Since Vanessa listened to her boss's advice, she rarely makes errors.

Another time, Bruce observed Vanessa handling an angry customer who was returning merchandise. Vanessa didn't allow the customer's rudeness to upset her. Bruce remarked, "Nice job, Vanessa. You really maintained your self-control with a tough customer." Like Bruce, your boss may informally comment on your work.

In addition, many businesses conduct formal **performance evaluations**, also called performance reviews, performance appraisals, or performance ratings. During a formal performance evaluation, an employee meets with his or her immediate supervisor. This meeting usually occurs once a year. Some typical purposes of performance evaluations are listed below.

Purposes of Performance Evaluation Meetings

- To recognize an employee's past achievements

- To judge an employee's progress

- To identify an employee's strengths and weaknesses

- To suggest ways for improving performance

▼ Practice

Interview someone you know who has a full-time job. (If you work full-time, you may "interview" yourself.) Find out how the person's performance is evaluated by his or her employer. Take notes during the interview and share the information with the rest of the class.

Evaluating Your Own Job Performance

How effective do you think you are at performing your job? You can assume personal responsibility for your own career success by honestly evaluating your strengths and weaknesses. Keep a written record of your accomplishments—job assignments you have completed especially well. In addition, take the initiative to correct problem areas before your boss calls them to your attention.

▼ Practice

On another sheet of paper, write the answers to the questions in the Self-Evaluation Questionnaire below. Think of specific situations that explain why you answered *yes* or *no*. Honest responses to these questions can also help you prepare for your performance evaluation with your boss.

If you aren't working right now, write about a job you once had. Or use questions 1, 2, 3, 4, 5, and 11 to evaluate your house work or another activity you perform.

Self-Evaluation Questionnaire

1. What job-related skills do you perform well?

2. What job-related skills do you want to improve?

3. Do you perform your assigned duties accurately?

4. Do you complete your assigned duties on time?

5. Do you consistently arrive at work on time?

6. Do you have a good attendance record?

7. Do you gossip or spread rumors?

8. Do you ask useful questions?

9. Do you actively participate at meetings?

10. Does your personal life interfere with your work?

11. Is your work area organized?

12. Do you limit the amount of time you spend socializing with coworkers?

13. Do you support your boss's decisions?

14. Do you avoid conflicts with your boss and coworkers?

15. Are you willing to work overtime to help your boss or coworkers?

Responding to Criticism

If a friend criticizes your driving, how do you respond?

- Do you get angry?

- Are your feelings hurt?

- Do you ignore the criticism?

In everyday life, many people react emotionally to other people's **criticisms**. However, responding to your boss's criticisms requires a different approach.

When your boss identifies a problem in your work performance, don't take the criticism personally or become discouraged. Assume your boss's intention is to help you do a better job. If you made a mistake, ask your boss what steps you should take to avoid the same mistake in the future. You can build your skills in responding to criticism by following the suggested guidelines below.

Responding to Criticism: Guidelines

- **Apologize for your mistakes.**
  Example: "I'm sorry I stapled the pages of the report in the wrong order. Next time I'll double-check my work."

- **Watch your nonverbal behavior.**
  Example: Frowning, avoiding eye contact, rolling your eyes, and hanging your head down convey a negative response to the criticism.

- **Don't respond defensively.**
  Example: Avoid saying "You're always picking on me" or "It wasn't my fault."

- **Don't change the subject.**
  Example: "I know some of the mailing labels fell off the packages, but I have a perfect attendance record."

- **Ask questions if you don't understand the criticism.**
  Example: "You say I've lost interest in my job. Could you tell me specific things I've done that have given you that impression?"

▼ Practice

Think of situations in which someone has criticized you or you have criticized someone else. Choose examples from your personal life and your job. How did you—or the other person—respond to the criticisms?

Directions: This activity will help you practice your skill in responding to criticisms about your work. Choose a partner to work with. Each of you will take turns playing the roles of a supervisor and an employee during an informal performance evaluation. Guidelines for both of these roles follow.

SUPERVISOR'S GUIDELINES

Imagine your partner is a new employee. You believe that he or she doesn't care enough about doing a good job. Your conclusion about your partner's work attitude is based on the following observations:

- Arrives late to work

- Refuses to work overtime

- Takes overly long coffee breaks

Think of specific examples that would support these observations. Then talk about these problem areas with your partner. During your discussion, remember to be helpful and understanding.

EMPLOYEE'S GUIDELINES

Pretend you are a single parent. You are having some difficulty balancing your commitment to your job and your commitment to your children. Your work is important to you, and you are determined to succeed. However, you are occasionally late and refuse to work overtime because of your children. During your coffee breaks, you have long phone conversations with your babysitter.

At your performance evaluation meeting, try to follow the guidelines on page 82. Listen carefully to your partner's criticisms. Then, when it is your turn to speak, do the following:

1. Convince your partner that you care about your job. Explain why working is important to you.

2. Respond to your partner's specific observations. *Briefly* explain that these problems stem from your responsibilities to your children.

3. Tell your partner how you intend to avoid these problems in the future.

During a performance evaluation your employer will comment on your work.

The Difficult Employee

Helen is the owner of the Magic Scissors, a beauty salon. Amy, one of her employees, is a very good hairstylist. Amy is a recent graduate of Alfredo's School of Hair Design, where she received excellent grades. Working at the Magic Scissors is Amy's first full-time job.

Helen has frequently praised Amy on the quality of her work. Amy's customers are also very pleased with the way she cuts their hair. In fact, Amy earns more money in tips than any other hairstylist in the beauty salon.

Despite Amy's technical skills, Helen believes that Amy has an "attitude problem." Amy always brags to the other hairstylists about her big tips. She complains about having to shampoo customers' hair. On several occasions, Amy has told Helen, "You should hire a shampoo girl. All the better salons have one." Amy complains about working on Saturdays, since it interferes with her social life. Amy is also dissatisfied with Helen's schedule for distributing paychecks. Helen issues paychecks twice a month, but Amy wants to be paid every week.

Amy became very defensive when Helen discussed these problems with her.

> **Amy:** I'm the best hairstylist in the salon. I'm never late for work. Why are you picking on me?
>
> **Helen:** I'm not picking on you, Amy. I know you're an excellent hairstylist. But you're missing my point. You need to improve your attitude. Your complaints about shampooing hair, working on Saturdays, and getting paid twice a month have a negative effect on the other hairstylists. You're too demanding. You simply can't expect everything here to run your way.
>
> **Amy:** I bet the other hairstylists have been talking to you behind my back. That figures. They're just jealous because they don't get big tips.
>
> **Helen:** You're not listening! I'm discussing your attitude, not the other hairstylists.

▼ For Discussion

1. What advice would you give Amy about accepting criticism?
2. Do you think Amy is too demanding? Give reasons to explain your answer.
3. Do you think a positive attitude is as important as technical skills in performing a job well? Give reasons to explain your answer.

Writing

Many jobs require writing skills.

Imagine that you are a police officer. You might write traffic tickets, jot down the license plate number of a speeding car, or file a report on an arrest. While you spend most of your time at work speaking and listening, writing is an important part of your job.

In this section, you will learn strategies for writing carefully and accurately, in everyday life and at work. Lesson 12 provides practice in filling out different kinds of forms. You will learn how to double-check for completeness.

Lesson 13 introduces the To Do list— a tool that helps you organize your work and manage your time more efficiently. You'll also learn how to avoid time wasters.

In Lesson 14, you will learn the purposes of memos and how to select the most important information to put in a memo.

Lessons 15 and 16 highlight the importance of business letters. In those lessons, you will learn how to set up a professional-looking business letter. You'll also practice writing different types of letters, such as complaint letters and request letters.

Lesson 17 shows how writing can be a crucial part of the job-search process. Topics in this lesson include responding to a want ad, writing a job application letter, filling out a job application, and taking brief notes to prepare for a job interview.

Transferring and Recording Information

Sarah is a secretary for Rite Wrecking Company, a business that demolishes buildings. Based on her boss's memos, she fills out forms for the wrecking crew. Shown below are a memo from Sarah's boss and an order form she filled out.

TO: Sarah Mason
FROM: Arlene Wagner *aw*
SUBJECT: Instructions for
Wrecking Order
DATE: February 19, 199__

Sarah, I have just confirmed a contract with the City Housing Authority to demolish a three-story apartment building located at 1331 West Wrightwood. The building has been vacant for the past year. It is a potential firetrap and is infested with rats.

Please fill out the form to give to the wrecking crew. Tell them to schedule the demolition for February 28.

WRECKING ORDER FORM

Authorized by: Arlene Wagner

Date of Demolition: February 28, 199__

Contractor's Name: City Housing Authority

Address of Building: 3131 West Wrightwood

Description of Building: 3-story vacant apartment

Special Precautions: Building is rat infested and a potential firetrap.

When the wrecking crew arrived at 3131 West Wrightwood, the workers were confused. There was a three-story apartment building, but it was in excellent condition. Tony, the wrecking crew supervisor, phoned Arlene Wagner and told her about the problem.

Arnold checked the contract and told Tony, "I'll say there's a problem. You're at the wrong address. The building you're supposed to wreck is 1331, not 3131, West Wrightwood. Come back right away. Meanwhile, I'll settle this thing with Sarah."

Talk About It

- Why is it important to double-check the accuracy of information recorded on a form?
- What do you think Alene will tell Sarah?
- Have you ever filled out a form inaccurately or incompletely? If so, explain what happened.

Forms in Everyday Life

Jerry Lambert was paying the monthly bill for his credit card. He quickly made out the following check.

JERRY LAMBERT
491 East Morris
Chicago, IL 60610

No. 131

Aug. 28 19*9*—

Pay to the
order of ___*National Bank MasterCard*___ $ *200.00*

___*Two hundred and*___ *00/100* DOLLARS

**National Bank
Chicago**

For _____ *Jerry Lambert*

As Jerry put the check into the envelope, he noticed the questions printed on the back of the envelope:

- Is the check made out for the correct amount?

- Did you make the check payable to National Preferred MasterCard?

- Did you write your account number on the check?

- Did you include the top portion of the monthly statement?

Jerry realized he hadn't followed the bank's guidelines for writing the check. He also compared his check with the top portion of his monthly statement.

Account Number	Payment Due Date	New Balance	Minimum Amount Due	Amount Paid
1321 405 302 415	09/4/9__	$1,531.67	$60.00	*$200.00*

▶ What information on Jerry's check is inaccurate or incomplete?

Jerry did not write "National Bank *Preferred* MasterCard" nor did he write his account number.

▶ Checks, as well as deposit and withdrawal slips, are examples of printed forms supplied by banks. What other types of forms have you filled out recently?

Guidelines: Filling Out Forms

- **Read the form first.** Identify the purpose of the form and the information you need to include.

- **Follow the instructions.** Listen carefully if someone orally explains the instructions for filling out the form. Otherwise, carefully follow the printed instructions on the form.

  Examples: Please print. Use pen only.

- **Record the information in the appropriate places.**

  Example: Name: _____ Powers, Jacob N. _____
  (last name, first name, middle initial)

- **Check your work for accuracy.** Double-check dates, numbers, and facts. Make sure the form is complete.

Filling Out an Order Form

Read the ad below. Pretend you want to buy at least two sets of bowls. Next, fill out the order form.

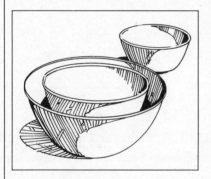

NEW!
Glass Bowls in Decorator Colors!

These nesting bowls will look terrific on your dinner table! Safe for microwave, oven, and freezer, these versatile bowls are easy to clean, too. Each set is only $9.95 plus $2.00 postage and handling. Comes in red, light blue, and yellow. One color per set.

SPECIAL OFFER!
Each additional set is just $8.95 plus $1.00 postage and handling.

The Kitchen Company • 21 Gorman Lane • Wikoski, VT 61742

No. of Sets	Color	Price per set	Postage and handling	Total

Enclosed is a check or money order for $ _____.

Name: _____

Address: _____

City: _____ State: _____ Zip Code: _____

Check the accuracy and completeness of your order form:

1. Did you remember to charge yourself only $8.95 for each additional set of bowls?

2. What is the amount you are enclosing?

3. Did you write your correct name and address?

Fill out the patient form below. If you prefer, fill in the form for someone else—a friend, relative, or imaginary character—and make up any information you don't know. After completing the form, choose a partner to work with. Exchange forms and check them for accuracy and completeness.

WASHINGTON MEDICAL CENTER
Patient Form

Please Print ● Use Pen Only

Name _____ Date _____
(last)   (first)   (middle initial)

Address _____
(street)   (city)   (state)   (zip code)

Phone (home) _____
(area code)

(work) _____
(area code)

Sex: ☐ male ☐ female   Date of Birth _____

Marital Status: ☐ single ☐ married ☐ divorced ☐ widowed

Number of children _____   Occupation _____

Do you have any medical problems? Please explain.

_____

Have you ever been hospitalized? Please explain.

_____

Do you smoke? ☐ Yes ☐ No

Do you have medical insurance? ☐ Yes ☐ No

(Fill out, if applicable)
   Name of insurance company _____

   Policy account number _____

Date of last medical visit _____
(month)   (year)

Name of previous physician _____

Telephone Message Forms

At your job, you will also transfer and record information onto printed forms. Sometimes you will record information that a coworker, boss, or customer gives you orally. In these cases, you will need to listen carefully. After you have filled out the form, you should check with the speaker to make sure you have recorded the information accurately.

When you take a telephone message, for example, you may need to complete forms like the one shown below. Remember to check the spellings of the callers' names and their phone numbers.

▼ Practice

Choose a partner to work with. First, read the dialogue aloud together. Take turns playing the roles of Jody, the caller, and Dale, the receiver of the call. As you play the role of the receiver, fill out the telephone message form that follows the script. (If you don't have a partner to work with, read the dialogue and fill out the message form.)

IMPORTANT MESSAGE

FOR _____

DATE _____ TIME _____ A.M. / P.M.

M _____

OF _____

PHONE _____
AREA CODE   NUMBER   EXTENSION

TELEPHONED		PLEASE CALL	
CAME TO SEE YOU		WILL CALL AGAIN	
RETURNED YOUR CALL		**URGENT**	

MESSAGE _____
_____
_____
_____
_____
_____

SIGNED _____

Dale: Archway Computer World, Dale Nowinski. May I help you?

Jody: Yes, this is Jody Stein from Hi-Tech Software. May I speak to Maggie Donaldson?

Dale: I'm sorry, but Maggie is on her lunch break now. May I take a message?

Jody: Yes, tell her I'd like to schedule a sales meeting with her. I'm sure she would be interested in seeing some of our latest software programs.

Dale: I'll give her the message. Ms. Stein, would you spell your last name for me and give me your phone number?

Jody: Sure, S-t-e-i-n. My number is 555-7111, extension 914.

Dale: That's S-t-e-i-n at 555-7111, extension 914.

Jody: Right. Thank you.

Dale: You're welcome. Good-bye.

Filling Out a Business Form

Below is a copy requisition form. Employees at C&R Corporation send this form to the company's copy center when they have large photocopying jobs. Read the form carefully.

C&R CORPORATION
COPY REQUISITION

Number of copies of each original needed _____

Number of originals (each side is an original) _____

☐ One-sided   ☐ Collated

☐ Two-sided   ☐ Collated and stapled

Copies are usually to be run on white paper. If you want colored paper, please specify color.

_____

Brief description of originals (title, opening words, etc.)

_____

Special instructions _____

_____

Copies needed by (date) _____ Time _____

Requested by _____ Date of request _____
     (print your name)

▼ Practice

A. Read aloud the following instructions about a job to send to the copy center and fill out the copy requisition on this page. If you are working with a class, ask a partner to read the instructions aloud while you write.

> "I typed a 10-page report entitled 'C&R Training Programs.' (*pause*) Submit the copy requisition today, October 11. (*pause*) I'd like 50 copies of the report by 9:30 A.M. on Friday, October 14. (*pause*) I want one-sided copies, collated. (*pause*) Under 'Special instructions,' write 'punch holes for a three-ring binder.' "

Ask the volunteer any questions you may have about the instructions. Then compare your filled-out forms with other students' forms.

B. If you are working, try to bring in some blank business forms from your job. Meet with a partner or partners and explain how to fill out these forms.

WORKING TOGETHER

Directions: This activity will give you practice in transferring and recording information onto a work schedule. Choose a partner to work with. Pretend that you operate a cleaning service together. You provide the following services for business customers: (1) carpet cleaning, (2) window washing, and (3) floor scrubbing and waxing.

Below is a list of next week's jobs.

Tues./Nelson's Menswear
1401 W. Webster
Phone: 555-0065
Acct. 0417/window washing

Fri./Paris Cafe
2106 N. Halston
Acct. 1238/window
washing, carpet cleaning
Phone: 555-4320

Thurs./Fiesta Restaurant
180 S. Ashland
floor scrubbing and waxing
Phone: 555-4610/Acct. 1328

Mon./Vivian's Hair Salon
4507 N. Higgins Rd.
Phone: 555-6777
window washing, floor
scrubbing and waxing
Acct. 0291

Working together, you and your partner will record the preceding information onto a work schedule. Use the following guidelines:

1. Carefully review the work schedule form below. Notice the code you should use for the types of services:

   C = carpet cleaning
   W = window washing
   F = floor scrubbing and waxing

2. Record the information in the appropriate places.

3. Check the form for accuracy and completeness. Your partner should read aloud the completed work schedule as you compare the information with the original notes.

		WORK SCHEDULE			
Day	Customer's Name and Address	Phone	Account Number	Type of Service*
Monday				
Tuesday				
Wednesday				
Thursday				
Friday				
*C = carpet cleaning W = window washing F = floor scrubbing and waxing				

The Job Application Form

James Randolph filled out a job application for the position of stock clerk at Save-U Supermarket. The store manager told James, "Please neatly *print* the information." Portions of James's application appear below.

Application for Employment

Date *December 10, 199—*

Name *James*   *Randolph*   *Winston*
       Last   First   Middle

Address *431 W. Bay*   *Los Angeles*   *Ca.*
       Street   City   State   Zip Code

Phone Number (   ) *555-7121*   Social Security Number *428-71-6501*
       Area Code

Employment Experience
(Start with your current or most recent job.)

Date (Month & Year)	Name and Address of Employer	Salary	Position	Reason for Leaving
From *9/87* To *10/88*	*Burger World Los Angeles*	*$3.25 / hour*	*counter clerk*	*went back to school*
From *1989* To *1990*	*Healthway Drug Store, Los Angeles*	*$3.50 / hour*	*stock clerk*	*out of business*
From *1990* To *1991*	*Greenway Nursing Home, Los Angeles*	*$4.50 / hour*	*maintenance*	*couldn't work night shift*

▼ For Discussion

1. Did James follow the oral and written instructions for filling out the job application? Give reasons to support your answer.

2. Do you think the store manager will consider hiring James? Give examples to explain your answer.

3. What advice would you give to James about filling out forms?

Writing To Do Lists

Dahlia and Sam Baxter both work full-time. They also have three children. Because Dahlia and Sam are so busy, they schedule their activities on their wall calendar. The calendar serves as an important reminder of things they have to do.

SUNDAY	MONDAY	TUESDAY	WEDNESDAY	THURSDAY	FRIDAY	SATURDAY
1 Grocery Shopping Laundry	2	3	4	5 Pick up dry cleaning	6	7 Mary's Birthday Party at 4:00 P.M.
8	9	10 Parent Teacher Meeting 7:00 P.M.	11	12	13	14 Church rummage sale
15	16	17	18 Take car in for a tune-up	19	20 Movie with the Warners 8:00 P.M.	21 Sam's dentist appt. 2:00 P.M.
22	23	24 Take Jenny to the library	25	26	27 Dinner at Mom's	28 Pay Bills
29	30 Gary's School Project due	31				

Talk About It

- What are the benefits of scheduling personal activities on a calendar?
- What activities have you forgotten to do because you didn't write them down?

Managing Your Time

Do you have a very busy schedule like Dahlia and Sam Baxter? If you work *and* take care of a family, you may experience difficulty balancing your work and your personal responsibilities. One way of striking a balance between the two is to gain control of your time.

▶ How much time does managing your personal responsibilities require? Fill out the chart below.

Responsibilities and Activities	Time Required (hours per week)
Cooking	_____
Laundry	_____
Housecleaning	_____
Yard work	_____
Paying bills	_____
Child care	_____
Family activities	_____
Leisure activities	_____
Add your own:	
_____	_____
_____	_____
_____	_____

Like the Baxters, you may find it helpful to schedule some of these responsibilities and activities on a wall calendar. You may also find it helpful to use a date book—a calendar in book form.

▼ Practice

To help you organize your time, schedule your personal activities for one week on the calendar below. Refer to the chart you filled out on page 96.

	Morning	**Afternoon**	**Evening**
Sunday			
Monday			
Tuesday			
Wednesday			
Thursday			
Friday			
Saturday			

Writing Lists

Another way of organizing your time is to write **lists**. For example, writing a grocery list helps you save time while you are shopping in the supermarket. You spend less time at the store deciding what you need or going back for forgotten items. Before you do your holiday shopping, you might write a list of friends and relatives and the gifts you want to buy them. Writing lists can also help you prepare for a party or plan a vacation.

▼ Practice

A. Preparing for a Party

Suppose you are planning to give a party. On the lines below, write a list of activities you would need to do to get ready for the party. Do not number them yet.

_____

_____

_____

Reread your list. What activity would you do first, second, and so on? Number the activities in the order you would complete them.

B. Planning a Vacation

Choose a partner to work with. Pretend the two of you are planning a trip. Decide on a place you both would like to visit.

First, work together to write a list of things you need to do to plan the travel arrangements. (Use another sheet of paper if you need more space.)

_____

_____

_____

Next, each of you write a list of things you will pack in your suitcase. (Use another sheet of paper if you need more space.)

_____

_____

_____

Writing To Do Lists

At your job, you need to manage your time efficiently and complete your assigned responsibilities on time. Writing a daily or weekly To Do list can help you become a more productive employee.

A **To Do list** is a written list you can use to organize your work. First, you list the required tasks you need to complete. Then you rank the tasks in the order in which you should complete them.

For example, Gail is a waitress at a restaurant in a large hotel. The restaurant manager has assigned Gail to work the breakfast shift. Gail has about one hour to get ready before the restaurant opens. Since this is Gail's first time on the breakfast shift, she quickly jots down everything she needs to do from 6 A.M. to 7 A.M.

Gail looks over the tasks on the list. She decides it would be most efficient to begin by preparing everything that needs to go on the tables. She plans to make the coffee next. She writes down the tasks in order on a To Do list.

Read Gail's final version of her To Do list below.

To Do List : Monday, Dec. 18

Rank	Description of Task	Completed
1.	Fill salt and pepper shakers	✓
2.	Fill containers with packages of jams, jellies, and honey	✓
3.	Fill containers with packages of sugar and sweeteners	✓
4.	Arrange pats of butter on ice	✓
5.	Make coffee	✓

▼ Practice

1. Is it a good idea for employees to show their To Do lists to their supervisors? Why or why not?

2. What do you think might have happened if Gail had *not* written a To Do list? Why?

Using Your Time Well

You have probably heard the familiar expression "time is money." At your job, you should consider time as money, so invest your time wisely. In other words, take control of the hours you spend at work and don't waste them.

Many employees do not use their hours at work well because they are not aware of their own time-wasting habits. For example, look at the picture of Floyd's office.

As you can see, Floyd's desk is messy and cluttered. He wastes time because he has difficulty finding the papers he needs. A messy and cluttered work area is a typical example of a time waster.

Listed below are some other common examples of time wasters at work:

- Arriving late to work
- Daydreaming
- Avoiding tasks that are boring or difficult
- Spending too much time talking to coworkers

▶ On the lines below, add your own examples of time wasters.

_____

_____

_____

Floyd's office

▼ Practice

Look again at the picture of Floyd's office. Based on the picture, answer the following questions.

1. What impression do you have of Floyd?

2. How would you describe Floyd's work habits?

3. Do you think Floyd has problems performing his job? Give reasons to explain your answer.

WORKING TOGETHER

Directions: This exercise will help you practice writing a To Do list. Choose a partner to work with. Each of you will write your own To Do list. Afterward, you and your partner will discuss your lists. Guidelines for completing these activities follow.

WRITING GUIDELINES

1. On a separate sheet of paper list 5 to 10 tasks you need to do on your next day at work. If you are not currently working, list 5 to 10 tasks from your home life that you need to accomplish by tomorrow night.

2. Review your list carefully. Next, rank each task in the order you plan to do it. Then complete the form below. (Note: You do not have to fill out the *Completed* column.)

PARTNERS' MEETING GUIDELINES

Discuss your To Do lists with each other. Explain your reasons for the rank you assigned each task. Invite your partner to ask questions about the tasks you described.

	TO DO LIST		
		Date _____	
Rank	Task	Time Required to Complete Task	Completed (✓)
1.			
2.			
3.			
4.			
5.			
6.			
7.			
8.			
9.			
10.			

Piling Up Paperwork

Irma is a medical technician at a hospital lab. Her favorite part of the job is working with patients. She knows how to calm people who are nervous about taking blood tests.

However, she dislikes doing the paperwork associated with her job. Irma is required to fill out the patients' insurance forms and the lab reports for blood tests. She puts the forms and reports in a basket on her desk.

To avoid doing the paperwork, Irma occupies her time with less important tasks. For example, when she's not busy with patients, she straightens her work area, which is already neat and organized. During her free time, she talks to her coworkers, whom she likes very much.

Irma waits to the last minute to complete the lab reports and the insurance forms. Doctors complain that they don't receive patients' test results soon enough. The hospital's billing department gets the insurance forms late and, occasionally, not at all. As a result, the billing department mistakenly charges some patients for the cost of their lab tests.

Over His Head

Nathan is an office assistant at a large law firm. He is responsible for filing and photocopying. Since he works for four lawyers, he has problems ranking the importance of the tasks they assign him. He writes a To Do list, but he is never quite sure which tasks he should do immediately and which tasks he can do later. As a result, Nathan is often behind in his filing and doesn't submit some of the photocopied materials on time.

▼ For Discussion

1. What suggestions would you make to Irma about managing her time?

2. At your job, do you ever put off doing certain tasks because they are boring or unenjoyable? If so, what are the effects? Give specific examples to explain your answer.

3. What do you think is the more important part of Irma's job—communicating effectively with patients or filling out forms? Give reasons to explain your answer.

▼ For Discussion

1. Is Nathan's problem with meeting deadlines entirely his fault? Give reasons to explain your answer.

2. Who should review Nathan's To Do list? Why?

3. What are the difficulties in working for more than one boss?

Writing Memos

Do you ever leave notes on your refrigerator door? Read the examples below.

A reminder

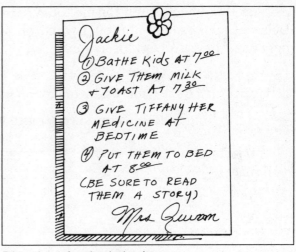

Directions for the babysitter

A thank-you note

A telephone message

Talk About It

- What kinds of notes do you write for your family members or roommates? Give specific examples.
- Have you ever forgotten to give someone a phone message? If so, describe what happened.
- When is a note a more effective way to communicate than a conversation?

Notes in Everyday Life

When you need to communicate with someone you live with, you probably have a face-to-face conversation. However, if that person is not at home, you might write a short note similar to the ones on page 13. These written messages take the place of conversations.

You might also write a note that restates information you already told the other person. For example, before Kathy left for work, she said to her husband, "Ron, would you pick up the dry cleaning for me today? Our jackets are at Deluxe Cleaners, 252 Clinton. I won't be home until 6:30 because I have to work overtime."

"Sure, Kathy, but would you leave a note on the refrigerator for me? You know me; otherwise, I'll forget."

▶ On the lines below, write Kathy's note to her husband.

_____

_____

_____

_____

Your note should restate Kathy's oral reminder. Putting the message in writing will help Ron remember the important details.

▼ Practice

On a separate sheet of paper, write a short note to a family member or roommate about each of the following situations. Use details from your own experience.

1. Write a phone message. Include the caller's name, phone number, and reason for calling.

2. Write a note giving a few simple directions.

3. Write a note thanking someone for doing you a favor.

Now check your notes:

- Are they neatly written?

- Do they contain all the necessary information?

- Are they brief and to the point?

Business Memos

Like a note, a **memo** is a written message, usually short and informal. Business memos are an efficient way for employees in the same workplace to communicate with each other. For instance, memos may serve to announce meetings, notify employees of changes in company policy, give simple directions, or make requests. Many workplaces use printed memo forms such as the one shown below.

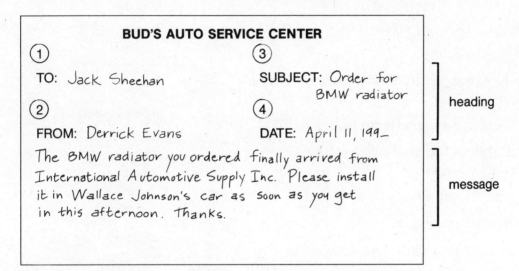

The memo form has two parts—the heading and the message. The **heading** consists of the following lines.

(1) The TO line identifies the person or group of people who receive the memo.

(2) The FROM line identifies the writer of the memo.

(3) The SUBJECT line briefly tells what the memo is about.

(4) The DATE line identifies when the memo is sent.

The **message** of the memo explains the subject line in more detail. The first sentence of the message usually states the main idea, and other sentences provide information related to the main idea.

▼ Practice

If you are working, recall some of the memos you have received at your job. Bring some in if you can. Then answer the following questions.

1. Who sent the memos? What were the memos about?

2. What action, if any, did the writers expect you take?

Planning the Memo

Before you actually write a memo, you should plan what you want to communicate. The following exercise will help you practice organizing information.

Imagine you run a mail-room. You are planning to write a memo announcing a change in mail-room procedures. Listed below are facts that you might want to include in your memo.

1. Your memo will be sent to all employees.

2. Today's date is August 3, 199___.

3. The mail room has changed its schedule for picking up outgoing mail.

4. The new schedule will go into effect on August 10.

5. A mail clerk will collect the mail twice in the morning and twice in the afternoon.

6. Morning Pickups: 9:30 and 11.

7. Afternoon Pickups: 1:30 and 4:30

8. Incoming mail is sorted into different categories.

▼ Practice

Reread the list of numbered statements above. Then choose the best answer for each question below.

1. Which of the following is the best summary for the SUBJECT line of the memo?

    a. Changes in Office Policy

    b. New Schedule for Mail Pickups

    c. Mail-room Clerk's Announcement

    d. Preparing the Mail

2. Which numbered statement from the list best explains the main idea of the memo?

    a. 3   b. 4   c. 6   d. 7

3. Which numbered statement from the list should you *not* include in the memo?

    a. 5   b. 6   c. 7   d. 8

Writing the Memo

Before writing a memo, it's a good idea to jot down all the facts you might include in it. Then go back and cross out the facts that are irrelevant. Put the relevant facts in a logical order. Then you are ready to write.

▼ **Practice**

A. Look back at the memo notes on page 106. Cross out the irrelevant facts. Then decide how you will order the relevant facts.

B. Using the information from the preceding page, write the memo.

TO: _____	DATE: _____
FROM: _____	SUBJECT: _____
(your name)	

_____

_____

_____

_____

_____

Morning Pickups	**Afternoon Pickups**
_____ A.M.	_____ P.M.
_____ A.M.	_____ P.M.

C. After you have completed writing the memo, evaluate its effectiveness. Use the following checklist as a guide. Then make any necessary changes that would improve the quality of your memo.

Memo Writing: Checklist

- Is the heading complete and accurate?

- Does the first sentence of the memo state the main idea?

- Is the written message clear, concise, and well organized?

- Is all the important information included? Are there any unnecessary details that should be omitted?

- Are all words spelled correctly?

Writing a Reminder Memo

Rosemary is a cashier at a supermarket. As she was leaving work on Thursday, she stopped at the customer-service desk to say good-bye to the store manager. "See you on Monday, Linda. Have a nice weekend."

Linda looked confused. "Aren't you coming in tomorrow?" she asked.

"No," Rosemary replied. "Don't you remember? I told you last week that I was taking tomorrow off as a personal day. You said it was OK. I'm moving into a new apartment over the weekend."

"Well, I vaguely remember that you mentioned something about moving, but I didn't realize you wanted to take a personal day. Rosemary, you should have written me a short memo about it, so I wouldn't forget. I hope I can find someone to cover for you tomorrow."

Memos are often useful for restating a spoken message. Memos can serve as written records or reminders of conversations with your boss or coworkers. When you want to remind them of something important, write a short memo summarizing what you said.

For example, below is a memo that Rosemary should have given to Linda.

TO: Linda Washington SUBJECT: Personal Day

FROM: Rosemary Martinez DATE: September 20, 199_

As we discussed today, I will be taking a personal day on Friday, September 28. I am moving into a new apartment that weekend.

▼ Practice

Imagine you are the owner of a small clothing store. You have told your employees that you plan to close the store on January 15 in honor of Dr. Martin Luther King, Jr.'s birthday. On a separate sheet of paper, write a brief memo reminding your employees of your decision. Be sure to use a heading.

Directions: This exercise will provide you with practice in writing memos. Choose a partner to work with. Each of you will write two memos—a request and a thank-you—independently. After you have completed the writing activity, you and your partner will meet to evaluate each other's memos.

WRITING GUIDELINES

1. Write a memo about each of the situations described below.

   Situation 1: Request Memo
   Ask your boss if you can take a personal day off to handle a private business matter. Be sure to specify the exact date of your absence in the memo.

   Situation 2: Thank-You Memo
   Imagine your boss approved your request to take a personal day. Thank a coworker who worked overtime to complete your work during your absence.

2. Copy the memo headings below on a separate sheet of paper. First, fill in the information for the heading. Then write the message. (If you are not working now, make up names for the boss and coworker.)

Situation 1

TO: _____   SUBJECT: _____
     (boss's name)   (topic of memo)

FROM: _____   DATE: _____
      (your name)   (month, day, year)

Situation 2

TO: _____   SUBJECT: _____
   (coworker's name)   (topic of memo)

FROM: _____   DATE: _____
      (your name)   (month, day, year)

PARTNERS' MEETING GUIDELINES

1. Meet with your partner and exchange the memos you have written.

2. Read each other's memos carefully. Evaluate the memos using the checklist on page 107.

3. Offer your partner suggestions for improving the memos. Don't be overly critical.

4. If necessary, rewrite your memos, making the changes that would improve their quality.

The Parking Memo

Andrea, Tyrone, and Mitch were sitting around a table in the employee cafeteria. They were discussing the following memo, which they had received in the morning.

HASTING PRODUCTS CORPORATION

TO: All Employees   SUBJECT: Disobeying Parking Policy

FROM: Ed Fritz, *EF*
Business Manager   DATE: July 15, 199__

    Many of you are abusing your parking privileges. You each have a reserved parking space. Nevertheless, you park in the most convenient spot available, so you can avoid long walks to the main entrance.

    Some of you even seem to have a problem reading signs. Certain parking spaces are clearly marked "Visitors Only" and "Handicapped Parking Only." Why do you insist on parking in these designated areas? Are you that inconsiderate?

    I want these parking violations to stop immediately. Those of you who continue to disobey our company's parking regulations will be punished.

Andrea: (*angrily*) Why did he send this memo to all employees? I can't believe *everyone* in the company is parking in someone else's space. I always park in my assigned space.

Tyrone: So do I. And the line about not knowing how to read really offends me. The business manager must think we're all stupid.

Andrea: I guess so. He also thinks we're lazy because we "avoid long walks." Oh, yeah, and we're "inconsiderate," too. A lot of people in my department thought this memo was really insulting.

Mitch: Well, of course, I got a copy of this memo too, and it doesn't even apply to me. I don't drive; I take the train to work. What bothers me about the memo is the threat of being punished.

▼ For Discussion

1. Do you agree or disagree with Andrea's, Tyrone's, and Mitch's opinions about the memo? Give reasons to explain your answer.

2. Do you think the memo will successfully motivate employees to follow parking regulations? Give reasons to explain your answer.

3. Why should a memo writer be aware of the readers' possible reactions?

4. How could the memo writer have worded the message in a way that would not have angered Andrea, Tyrone, and Mitch?

Organizing Business Letters

Marty and Ed were standing outside their apartment building. They were watching construction workers laying the pavement for a city parking lot across the street.

Marty: That new parking lot is going to be a real nuisance. There's enough traffic in this neighborhood already.

Ed: I'll say. The store owners around here are probably happy, though. They know it will really boost their business.

Marty: Sure, but meanwhile we'll have to put up with all the noise and the congestion. I guess our opinion is in the minority.

Ed: What do you mean?

Marty: Don't you remember getting a letter from the city commissioner last year?

Ed: Oh, yeah, I remember. So what?

Marty: Well, the commissioner's letter said that the city was planning to build a parking lot. Anyone who was opposed to the plan was to notify the commissioner in writing. So naturally, I wrote the commissioner a letter explaining why I was against the parking lot.

Ed: I suppose I should have written a letter too, but it probably would have been a waste of time.

Marty: No, that's not true. Letters can have a lot of influence. In another area of the city, restaurant owners wanted to open beer gardens. You know—those bars that serve liquor outdoors in the summer? Well, people in that neighborhood started a letter-writing campaign. The beer gardens were banned because the city commissioner received so many complaint letters.

Ed: OK, maybe you're right. I guess I just avoid writing letters. I'm not sure what to say or how to say it.

Marty: Writing a letter isn't that big of a deal. Next time, call me up. I took a course in writing business letters at the adult community center. I'd be glad to give you some pointers.

Ed: Thanks. I'm going to take you up on that offer.

Talk About It

- Marty told Ed, "Letters can have a lot of influence." Do you *agree* or *disagree* with this statement?
- Have you ever sent a business letter? Why did you write it? What was the effect of writing the letter?

The Business Letter Format

The general appearance of a **business letter** is very important. A reader *sees* a letter before he or she reads it. A typed letter makes a better impression than a handwritten one. (If you do not type, ask you instructor for information on how to learn.) In any case, the letter should be neat and should follow a format.

The letter below is an example of a full-block format. Notice how the six essential parts of the letter are arranged on the page.

---

(1) 312 West Washington Street
Baltimore, MD 21218
July 1, 199___

(2) Mr. Martin Nichols
1076 West Washington Street
Baltimore, MD 21218

(3) Dear Mr. Nichols:

(4) The city of Baltimore is planning to build a parking lot on the corner of Washington and Central streets. As your city commissioner, I am interested in knowing whether residents of your precinct approve of this plan.

If you have any objections to building the parking lot, please notify me in writing within the next two weeks. A special panel will review all residents' letters before a final decision is made.

Remember, your opinion counts.

(5) Sincerely yours,

(6) *Ray Collins*

Ray Collins
City Commissioner

---

(1) **Heading**   (3) **Salutation**   (5) **Complimentary close**

(2) **Inside Address**   (4) **Body**   (6) **Signature**

More About Letter Parts

Refer to the letter on page 112 as you read the explanation of the letter parts.

(1) The **heading** consists of the letter writer's address and the date.

(2) The **inside address** includes the name and address of the person or company receiving the letter. Use the abbreviation *Ms.,* or *Mr.* before the person's name.

(3) The **salutation** is the conventional greeting used in letters. Begin the salutation with the word *Dear,* the abbreviation *Ms.,* or *Mr.,* and the person's last name. Put a colon (:) after the name.

(4) The **body** consists of the written message organized into paragraphs.

(5) The **complimentary close** is a polite expression that concludes the letter. Some examples of complimentary closing lines are *Sincerely, Sincerely yours,* and *Truly yours.*

(6) The **signature** follows the complimentary close. Below your signature, your name should be typed (or neatly printed, if the letter is handwritten).

▼ Practice

A. Write the letter of the correct definition next to the term.

_____ **1.** heading

_____ **2.** inside address

_____ **3.** salutation

_____ **4.** body

_____ **5.** complimentary close

_____ **6.** signature

a. the written message

b. a polite expression that concludes the letter

c. the letter writer's address and the date

d. the handwritten name of the letter writer

e. the word *Dear* followed by the name of the person receiving the letter

f. the name and address of the person receiving the letter

B. Find a business letter you have received at home. Label the six essential parts.

Capitalization and Punctuation

As you already noticed, you should follow certain rules for capitalizing and punctuating the parts of a business letter. Apply the following **capitalization** and **punctuation rules** when you write a business letter.

Capitalize

- the words *North*, *South*, *East*, and *West* in the street address

  Examples: 421 North Broadview Avenue
  1001 South State Street

- the names of streets

  Examples: Winston Boulevard   Sheridan Road

- the names of cities

  Examples: Detroit   San Francisco

- the two-letter abbreviations for states

  Examples: MD (Maryland)   CA (California)

- the names of the months

  Examples: October 23, 199___   August 10, 199___

- the first word of every sentence

  Example: We have approved your credit card application for our store. You will receive your Bargain World credit card within two weeks.

- the first word only in the complimentary close

  Examples: Sincerely yours,   Truly yours,

Use a Comma

- between the city and the state

  Examples: Chicago, IL   Newark, NJ

- between the day of the month and the year

  Example: October 22, 199___

- after the complimentary close

  Example: Sincerely,

Use a Colon

- after the salutation

  Examples: Dear Mr. Brown: Dear Ms. Hernandez:

▼ Communication Tip

Except for state abbreviations and Mr., Ms., and Mrs., avoid using abbreviations in business letters.

Most of the business letter parts below contain errors in capitalization, punctuation, spelling, or abbreviation style. Write the corrections on the lines provided. If there is no error, leave the line blank. You may use a dictionary.

1. 432 N. Moss Rd.

New orleans, LA 70119

September 6 199__

2. Mr. Jim Lowell

Lowell's Muffler Shop

6034 north Clark Street

Louisville Ky 40201

3. Dear Mr. Lowell,

4. Truely Yours;

5. 120 w. Fulton avenue

Dallas; TX 75080

november 3, 199__

6. Ms. Carol Andrews

1400 West Bucaro Avenue

Dallas TX 75080

7. Dear Ms. Andrews;

8. congratulations! you

have just won a free

trip to Jamaica.

9. sincerely yours—

Addressing Envelopes

The person who receives your letter will notice the
envelope first. Therefore, the appearance of your envelope
is also important. Both the return address and mailing
address should be neatly typed. (If you must write them,
use printing, not cursive handwriting.) Type the return
address in the upper left-hand corner of the envelope.
Begin typing the mailing address in the center. The
mailing address matches the inside address of your letter.

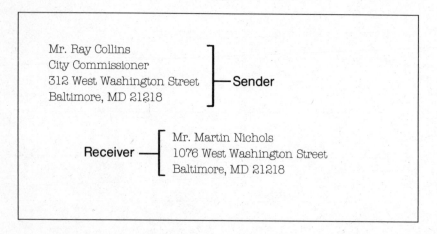

You have probably already noticed that you use the state
abbreviation for addresses both in the letter and on the
envelope. For your reference, here is the U.S. Postal
Service's list of state abbreviations.

Alabama	AL	Kentucky	KY	North Dakota	ND
Alaska	AK	Louisiana	LA	Ohio	OH
Arizona	AZ	Maine	ME	Oklahoma	OK
Arkansas	AR	Maryland	MD	Oregon	OR
California	CA	Massachusetts	MA	Pennsylvania	PA
Colorado	CO	Michigan	MI	Rhode Island	RI
Connecticut	CT	Minnesota	MN	South Carolina	SC
Delaware	DE	Mississippi	MS	South Dakota	SD
District of Columbia	DC	Missouri	MO	Tennessee	TN
Florida	FL	Montana	MT	Texas	TX
Georgia	GA	Nebraska	NE	Utah	UT
Hawaii	HI	Nevada	NV	Vermont	VT
Idaho	ID	New Hampshire	NH	Virginia	VA
Illinois	IL	New Jersey	NJ	Washington	WA
Indiana	IN	New Mexico	NM	West Virginia	WV
Iowa	IA	New York	NY	Wisconsin	WI
Kansas	KS	North Carolina	NC	Wyoming	WY

Directions: This exercise will give you practice using a business letter format. Choose a partner to work with. Read the contents of the business letter below and arrange the letter parts on the lines that follow. Use the full-block format as shown on page 112.

1. The person letter writer is Juan Cabrera. He lives at 462 North Shady Lane, Evanston, Illinois. The zip code is 60201.

2. Use today's date in the heading.

3. Juan is sending the letter to Yolanda Stone. She works at Bradley Realty, 800 South Ridge Avenue, Evanston, Illinois. The zip code is 60201.

4. This is the body of Juan's letter:

Paragraph 1: I will not be renewing my lease because I am moving out of town. However, my moving date is June 30, and the lease expires May 31. Would it be possible for me to stay the extra month?

Paragraph 2: I look forward to your response. Thank you for your help.

5. Juan uses the complimentary close *Sincerely yours.*

_____

_____

_____

_____

_____

_____

_____

_____

_____

_____

_____

_____

_____

_____

_____

The Request Letter

Jan. 9

Mr. Michael
Swift Messenger Service

Please send me your notes for your messenger service. My boss wants them. Also what are your delivery hours? Do you deliver on weekends? Just call me up and tell me, or send me a letter, or whatever.

Judy Barton

▼ For Discussion

1. Why do you think the visual appearance of a letter is important?
2. What parts of the business letter are missing or incomplete?
3. Will Mr. Michaels be able to respond to this letter? Give reasons to explain your answer.

The Job Application Letter

Stuart Bowie
Phoenix, Ariz., 85017

Monday, Aug. 1
Eugene Kessler
561 N. Chesterton, Phoenix

Eugene Kessler—
The want ad in the newspaper said I should write to you. You're looking for someone to answer phones and greet visitors at your company—also to take messages. You wanted someone with experience and I have a lot of it. I answer phones, take messages, and greet visitors very well. I am responsible and a hard worker. You wanted the names and phone numbers of three people I've already worked for. Mr. York at 555-3200, Mr. Wright at 555-1671, Mrs. Jonas at 555-2666.

Stuart Bowie
Phone—555-4141

▼ For Discussion

1. Based on the letter, do you think Eugene Kessler will interview Stuart Bowie for the job? Give reasons to explain your answer.
2. Are the letter parts arranged in an easy-to-read format? Find examples to support your answer.
3. Do the letter parts include all the necessary information? Are any letter parts missing? Give examples to support your answer.

Writing Business Letters

Brad and Emily Conelly had been saving for a weekend trip to celebrate their fifth anniversary. They flipped through the travel section of the newspaper and spotted the following ad:

MAKE LAKE GENEVA YOUR GETAWAY!

Spend your vacation at Bayview Lodge.
• Luxurious resort at affordable prices
• Whirlpool and sauna
• Swimming, water skiing, and fishing
Weekend special: 3 days, 2 nights for $120

Call for reservations today!
(800) 555-7059

"Emily, didn't Joyce and Trevor go to Bayview Lodge last year?" Brad asked.

"Yes," Emily replied. "They had a wonderful time. And the rates are within our budget. Why don't you call and make reservations?"

"Sounds like a good idea. I'll call right now."

Three weeks later, Emily and Brad drove to Lake Geneva. However, when they arrived at Bayview Lodge, they received an unpleasant surprise.

"I'm sorry, Mr. Conelly," said the lodge clerk. "There is no record of your reservations, and there are no other vacancies."

"Wait a minute," said Emily. "Five days after my husband called, we received a letter from the lodge confirming our reservations." She pulled an envelope out of her purse and handed it to the clerk.

The clerk frowned as he read through the letter and then looked up. "Will you excuse me for a moment?" he said as he left the desk and opened a door marked OFFICE.

Several minutes later, he returned with a smile on his face. "I have good news. It turns out that our honeymoon suite is still available, and the manager would like to invite you to stay in it at no extra charge."

"That *is* good news," said Brad. "I think we're ready for a second honeymoon."

Talk About It

• Why was the lodge suddenly able to find a vacancy?
• What are the advantages of writing letters to confirm what was said in a phone conversation?

Business Letter Style

▶ Do you write personal letters to friends or relatives? On the lines below, write part of a letter to a friend or relative who lives out of town.

Dear _____ ,

_____

_____

_____

_____

_____

_____

_____

_____

You probably write personal letters to tell someone about your latest experiences. You might describe an event in great detail or try to make the reader laugh.

Writing business letters is different from writing personal letters. The person who receives your business letter probably doesn't know you. Generally, you write business letters because you want your reader to take a specific action.

Examples:

- Cancel a magazine subscription

- Correct an error in your bank balance

- Grant a job interview

- Send merchandise you ordered

▶ On the line below, write your own example.

_____

Business letters are clear, concise, and accurate. Your reader should not have to second-guess your reason for writing. Business letters are also courteous. Your reader should not react angrily to your choice of words.

▼ **Characteristics of Business Letters**

Clear	Courteous
Concise	Accurate

The Writing Process

Business letter writing, like other forms of writing, is a process consisting of three related steps:

Step 1

Planning
the Message

Step 2

Writing
the Message

Step 3

Revising
the Message

As you learned in Lesson 15, the body of a business letter consists of the written message—the main points you want to communicate to the reader. Planning helps you organize your thinking *before* you begin to write the message.

Imagine the reader as he or she reads your letter. Will the reader understand why you are writing? Does the letter include all the information the reader needs to know? Does the letter clearly state what action, if any, the reader should take? Keeping these questions in mind, follow the guidelines below for planning a business letter.

Guidelines: Planning a Business Letter

- **List all the facts and details you wish to include.** For example, suppose you wanted to send a reservation to a lodge or hotel. You might include the following details: (1) the type of room, (2) the rate or cost, (3) the number of people, and (4) the dates of your arrival and departure.

- **Check the list of details for completeness.** Make sure your list includes all the necessary information you wish to communicate. For example, in a reservation letter, you might want to add an additional point—a request for a confirmation letter.

- **Organize the details in the order you want to write them.** Arrange the information so that the reader clearly understands the message. Generally, you should begin your letter with your reason for writing. Conclude your letter with the action you want your reader to take.

On the next three pages, you will read about how Michael Kruger planned, wrote, and revised a business letter.

Planning a Business Letter

Michael Kruger received a letter from Sheryl Rhodes, an agent from Safeway Auto Insurance Company:

Dear Mr. Kruger:

Your six-month premium of $500 for your auto insurance is now past due. If we do not receive your payment by the end of the month, your auto insurance policy will be terminated.

Michael had paid the bill on time, and he had a canceled check from the bank to prove it. Michael decided to write a letter to Sheryl Rhodes about the error. To plan the letter, Michael wrote the following notes.

Inside Address : Ms. Sheryl Rhodes,
　　　　　　　　Safeway Auto Insurance Company,
　　　　　　　　2430 N. Kenmore, Chicago, IL,
　　　　　　　　60614
Include these points : - Say error was made
　　　　　　　　　　- Enclose photocopy of cancelled check
　　　　　　　　　　- Date of check 6/13
　　　　　　　　　　- Received letter on 7/10 about not
　　　　　　　　　　　paying

Michael reread his notes and added these details:

- check amount $ 500.
- Insurance policy account # 3674
- tell Rhodes to correct mistake

▼ Practice

1. Did you ever receive a letter stating you did not pay a bill on time? If so, explain the situation and your response.

2. If you were Michael, would you call Sheryl Rhodes or write her a letter? Give reasons to explain your answer.

3. Did Michael list all the necessary facts and details to include in the letter? Give examples to support your answer.

4. Did Michael organize the details in the order he wanted to write them? Give examples to support your answer.

The First Draft

After Michael planned the message, he was ready to write his first draft. He didn't worry about grammar or spelling for now. His main purpose was to get his sentences down on paper.

▶ Read Michael's notes below. What is your opinion of them?

July 12, 199_

Ms. Sheryl Rhodes
Safeway auto insurance company
2430 N. Kenomore Ave.
Chicago, IL 60614

Ms. Rhodes,

Why are you going to cancel my insurence policy #3674? Don't you know it's against Illinois law for a car owner not to have auto insurance. If I drive my car without insurance, I could get arrested. You wrote me a letter on July 10 saying I didn't pay my $500 premium, but I can prove that I did. You made the error, so make the correction.

I'm enclosing a copy of the canseled check I sent you. The amount on the check is $500. So you see, I did pay my check on time because the date on the check is June 13. My account number is 3674. Make sure your records show I paid the $500 premium.

Sincerely,
Michael Kruger

As Michael read his first draft, he noticed that the letter sounded angry, confused, and rambling. It contained unnecessary details about the Illinois auto insurance law, and it repeated certain facts, such as his account number and the premium amount. Michael also found misspelled words and mistakes in capitalization.

▼ Practice

1. What information should Michael delete from the letter?

2. How do you think Sheryl Rhodes would respond if she received this draft of Michael's letter?

3. Find some examples in the letter of misspelled words, missing words, or mistakes in capitalization.

The Final Draft

Revising involves making any changes that will improve the effectiveness of your letter. Michael revised his letter, correcting the problems he had previously identified. He also decided to mention that he would follow up the letter with a phone call. He wrote one last draft and then the typed letter.

3042 North Southport Avenue
Chicago, IL 60657
July 12, 199___

Ms. Sheryl Rhodes
Safeway Auto Insurance Company
2430 North Kenmore Avenue
Chicago, IL 60614

Dear Ms. Rhodes:

According to your letter of July 10, you did not receive my six-month premium for my insurance policy. However, I did send you a check, dated June 13, for $500. ———— reason for writing

Enclosed is a photocopy of my canceled check. My policy account number is 3674. ———— important details

Please correct this error as soon as possible. I will call you in a couple of days to make sure my payment has been accurately recorded. ———— reader's action & writer's follow-up

Sincerely,

Michael Kruger

Michael Kruger

▶ Evaluate Michael's letter using the following checklist.

Writing Evaluation Checklist

☐ Is the information clear and concise?

☐ Is the information complete and accurate?

☐ Does the letter show respect toward the reader?

☐ Are all the necessary parts of the letter included?

☐ Is the format correct?

Focusing on the Reader

Michael's letter was effective because it clearly explained information to the reader, Sheryl Rhodes. Like Michael, when you write business letters, you must know what to say and how to say it. To accomplish this goal, the written message you send should focus on the reader, the receiver. After you write a letter, ask yourself, "How will it sound to the reader?"

Read the following excerpts from two business letters.

> That VCR I bought at your store last week is a piece of garbage. It doesn't rewind the videotape, and the remote control is no good. I demand a refund.

> Last week I bought a Power-Tech video recorder at your store. The rewind button and the remote control don't work. According to your store policy, I'm eligible for a refund.

► Which of these written messages would you rather receive? Why?

As you probably noticed, in the first excerpt, the writer expresses anger toward the reader. However, in the second excerpt, the writer politely states his complaint to the reader.

The characteristics below describe a writer whose written message focuses on the reader.

- Understands the reader's point of view
- Uses language familiar to the reader
- Shows respect toward the reader
- Encourages a favorable reaction from the reader

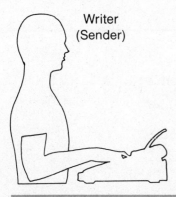
Writer
(Sender)

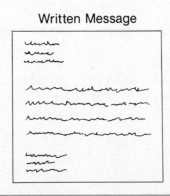
Written Message

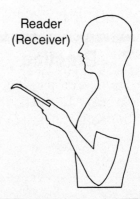
Reader
(Receiver)

Reporting a Complaint

Have you ever been dissatisfied with a product you purchased or had repaired? If so, as a customer, you have the right to report your complaint. Read the following form letter and notice the information you should include in a complaint letter.

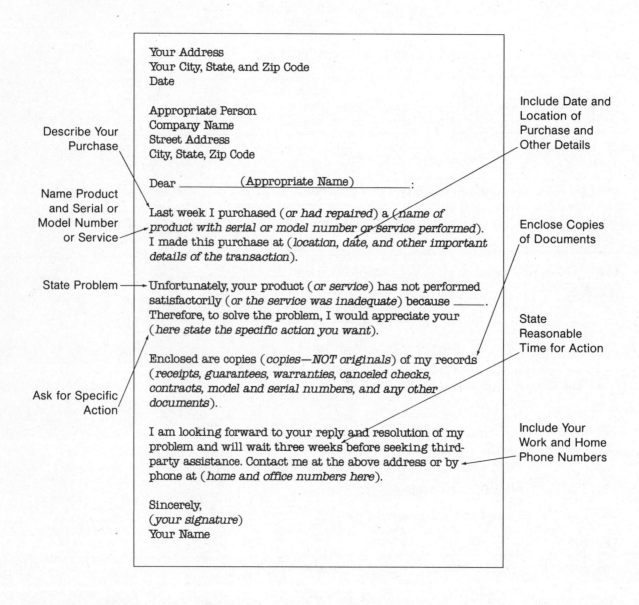

▼ Practice

Think of a product you bought that you were dissatisfied with. Complete the form letter on page 127 with the appropriate information. Use imaginary details if you do not recall the actual details.

_____
(your street address)

_____
(your city, state, and zip code)

_____
(date)

_____
(name of store manager)

_____
(name of store)

_____
(street address)

_____
(city, state, and zip code)

Dear _____:

Last week I purchased _____.
                      (name of product and serial number)

I made this purchase at _____.
                (location of the purchase)

Unfortunately, your product has not performed satisfactorily because _____

_____.
(state the problem with the product)

Therefore, to solve the problem, I would appreciate _____

_____.
(ask for the specific action you want—an exchange, a refund, and so on)

Enclosed are copies of _____.
              (name two documents you are enclosing)

I am looking forward to your reply and resolution of my problem and will wait three

weeks before seeking third-party assistance. Please contact me at the above address or by

phone at _____.
       (your phone number)

Sincerely,

_____
(signature

_____
(printed name)

After you have completed the form letter, answer the following questions.

1. Are the details clear and complete?

2. Did you offer a reasonable solution to the problem you described?

Writing a Request Letter

Michele Lorenz noticed the following ad in a magazine:

"Guide to Women's Employment Rights." This useful manual outlines women's rights on the job. To order, send a check for $7.95 to Bookworks Publishing, 5905 S.E. Forest Way, Seattle, WA 98145.

Michele works full-time as a nurse's aide at a hospital. Recently, she and her coworkers were discussing their legal rights as health-care workers. Michele thought this manual could provide her with important information. Consequently, she wrote a letter requesting it.

First, she jotted down some notes to help her plan and organize her letter. Her notes are shown at right.

Next, Michele wrote a first draft and made revisions. The final draft of her request letter appears below.

WHY: To request copy of publication

WHAT: "Guide to Women's Employment Rights" published by Bookworks Publishing, $7.95

HOW: letter and enclosed check payable to Bookworks Publishing

WHEN: As soon as possible?

WHERE: Send to Bookworks Publishing 5905 S.E. Forest Way, Seattle, Washington 98145

---

612 South Monroe Street
Brooklyn, NY 11201
January 16, 199___

Bookworks Publishing
5905 S.E. Forest Way
Seattle, WA 98145

Dear Publications Manager:

Please send me a copy of "Guide to Women's Employment Rights." As requested in your magazine ad, I am enclosing a check for $7.95.

I look forward to receiving this publication as soon as possible. Thank you.

Sincerely,

Michele Lorenz

Michele Lorenz

Like Michele, you also might want to write a request letter to get published materials, to order merchandise, or to ask for information. Follow the suggestions below for writing your request letter.

- Clearly state your request.
- Include necessary background information.
- Enclose the payment (if applicable).
- Conclude the letter courteously.

WORKING TOGETHER

Directions: This activity will give you practice in writing a request letter. Choose a partner to work with. Each of you will write a request letter independently. After you have completed the writing activity, you and your partner will meet to evaluate each other's letters. Guidelines for both of these activities follow.

WRITING GUIDELINES

1. Cut out a newspaper or magazine ad that tells you to write for more information about a product or service.

2. Plan a letter to the company and request a catalog, booklet, brochure, or other published information. Jot down some notes on the lines below.

   Title of publication _____

   _____

   Cost _____

   Method of payment _____

   Mailing address _____

   _____

   _____

3. On a separate sheet of paper write the first draft of your letter. Arrange the letter parts—heading, inside address, salutation, body, complimentary close, and signature—using the full-block format. Refer to Michele's letter page 128 as a model. Use the salutation *Dear Publications Manager.*

PARTNERS' MEETING GUIDELINES

1. You and your partner should exchange your advertisements and your request letters.

2. Read your partner's ad and letter carefully. Evaluate the letter using the checklist below.

   ☐ Is the request clearly stated in the first sentence?

   ☐ Is all the necessary information included?

   ☐ Is the letter well organized and clear?

   ☐ Does the letter contain correct spelling, punctuation, and capitalization?

3. Based on your evaluation, offer your partner suggestions that might improve the letter. Don't be overly critical.

4. Write the final draft of your letter, making any changes that would improve its quality. If possible, type the letter.

Following Up a Phone Call

Nadine read her bank's monthly statement for her checking account. She noticed the balance was incorrect, and she called a customer-service representative at the bank to complain.

Molly: Lincoln Bank Customer Services, Molly Weber.

Nadine: Hello, my name is Nadine Woods. I'd like to report an error in my checking account balance.

Molly: May I have your checking account number?

Nadine: Yes—6-0-4-2-9.

Molly: Ms. Woods, I've called up your account on the computer. What is the error?

Nadine: I was incorrectly charged with a $100 withdrawal from an automated teller machine on June 1. The first time I tried to get the $100, the withdrawal was denied. On the second try, I received the $100. However, as you can see on my statement, I've been charged with two $100 withdrawals instead of one.

Molly: I'm sorry that this happened. So that we can correct the error, please send me a letter describing what happened. State the address of the automated teller machine and the date you made the withdrawal. Include your checking account number, and enclose a copy of both transaction receipts.

Nadine: OK, but it's your fault the error was made.

Later that day Nadine wrote the following letter.

Dear Ms. Weber:

My checking account number is 60429, and you made an error on my monthly statement. I was incorrectly charged with a $100 withdrawal from an automated teller machine. So credit my balance with the $100 right away. The automated teller machine I used is located at 2901 North Western Avenue. Fix the mistake immediately, since it's your fault.

Sincerely,
Nadine Woods

▼ For Discussion

1. Did Nadine listen carefully to Molly's instructions for writing the letter? Give reasons to explain your answer.

2. Do you think Nadine planned what she wanted to say *before* she wrote the letter? Why or why not?

3. Based on Nadine's letter, will Molly be able to correct the error in Nadine's checking account? Give reasons to explain your answer.

Employment Communications

Ruth and Vera are eating lunch at a restaurant. Vera is discussing her new job as a phone salesperson.

Ruth: Congratulations! You must be excited about your new job.

Vera: I am excited. I think I'll be pretty good at phone sales because I enjoy talking to people. I hope I'll enjoy going to an office every day. Like you, I've been home raising my kids for the last few years.

Ruth: I wish I could be as confident as you are. Next year I plan to work full-time, too, and I'm pretty nervous about the whole idea.

Vera: At first, I was pretty nervous, too, but that workshop at the community center really helped me. My teacher gave me some good advice.

Ruth: Like what?

Vera: Pretty much the basics of looking for a job. We practiced filling out job applications and spent a lot of time on interviewing techniques.

Ruth: That's what worries me—going on

Interviewing can be the hardest part of looking for a job.

an interview. I haven't gone on a job interview for over three years.

Vera: I thought interviewing was the hardest part of looking for a job. I know I blew the first couple of interviews because I felt so uncomfortable. After a while, though, it got easier. My last interview for the phone-sales job went very smoothly. I knew the interviewer was pleased with the way I answered his questions. After the interview, he showed me around the office and introduced me to my new coworkers. They all seemed friendly.

Ruth: That's great! I can't wait to hear about how you like your new job.

Talk About It

- Do you think interviewing is the hardest part of looking for a new job? Why or why not?
- Why do you think Ruth feels nervous about looking for a new job?
- Why are communication skills important in finding a job? Give specific examples to support your answer.

Background Notes

When you apply for a job, the employer will be interested in learning about your **background** and **skills**. You may have to provide this information by filling out a job application form, writing a job application letter, or providing other types of written material. You may also need to provide information orally in interviews over the telephone or in person.

Before you apply for jobs, it is helpful to make up a set of notes that include the information employers are likely to want. You can keep this set of notes, add to it as you acquire more experience, and refer to it again and again. It is much easier to use your notes than to try to remember a lot of detailed information off the top of your head.

▼ Practice

Make up a set of background notes for yourself. Include all of the following information. For the first three categories, list your experience in time order from most recent to earliest.

1. **Education:** Names and addresses of schools or special programs you attended; dates you attended; diplomas, degrees, or certificates you earned

2. **Work Experience:** Names and addresses of every workplace; dates you worked there; job titles and responsibilities in each workplace; wages or salaries you earned; reasons you left

3. **Volunteer/Community Experience:** Names and addresses of any volunteer or community program you participated in; dates you were active; your responsibilities

4. **References:** Names and addresses of friends and former supervisors and coworkers who are willing to serve as your references

Keep your notes and update them as necessary.

Responding by Phone to a Want Ad

Jeanette Pearson had been unemployed for two months and was eager to find a new job. She looked through the Sunday newspaper's Job Guide and found the ad shown at the right.

Before Jeanette contacted Sam Graves, she wrote down his name and number. She also consulted her background information notes and wrote down the job information she thought Mr. Graves would want. Jeanette referred to her notes during her phone conversation with Sam Graves:

> **CAFETERIA SERVERS**
> Full-time
> $6.00/hr. plus benefits.
> Call Sam Graves, 555-8100
> T&G Manufacturing
> Company
> 3100 West Summit,
> Lincolnwood

> Mr. Graves / 555-8100
> - Interested in applying for job as cafeteria server
> - Worked for 3 years as cafeteria server at
>   Kennedy Elementary School, May '88 — last June
>   (lost job — school closed because of low enrollment)

Sam: Sam Graves, cafeteria manager.

Jeanette: Hello, my name is Jeanette Pearson. I'm interested in applying for the job of cafeteria server. I saw your want-ad in last Sunday's Job Guide.

Sam: Do you have previous experience as a cafeteria worker?

Jeanette: Yes, I was a cafeteria server at Kennedy Elementary School for three years.

Sam: And why did you leave that job?

Jeanette: The school closed last June because of low enrollment. That's why I'm looking for another food-service job.

Sam: Are you available for an interview this Thursday at 9 A.M.?

Jeanette: Yes. That would be fine.

Sam: We're located at 3100 West Summit in Lincolnwood. Go in the main entrance and stop at the receptionist's desk. She'll give you a job application to fill out, and then we'll have our interview.

Jeanette: (*taking notes*) I'll be looking forward to meeting you this Thursday morning. Thank you, Mr. Graves.

When you call someone to apply for a job, use Jeanette's approach as a model.

- Plan your call in advance.
- Write notes about your qualifications or job experience.
- Introduce yourself, and immediately say that you want to apply for the job.
- Identify where you learned about the job opening.

The Job Application Letter

Some want-ads request that interested individuals send a job application letter. The purpose of a job application letter is to summarize your qualifications and to request an interview.

For example, Steven Foley sent a letter in response to the ad shown at the right.

Use Steven's letter below as a model for your own application letter.

212 East Dewey Lane
Boston, MA 02115
February 15, 199___

Personnel Director
Dunn & Hayes
321 Lexington Road
Boston, MA 02115

Dear Personnel Director:

I would like to apply for the position of office clerk at your law firm. My qualifications meet your job requirements described in the Boston Tribune want ad. — Apply for job/State job title and source of ad

I worked for over a year as a clerk at KWIK Copy Center in Boston, where I photocopied both large and small jobs for business customers. I often worked overtime to meet the deadlines for these jobs. — Summarize qualifications

May I have an interview at your convenience? Please contact me at 555-3000. I look forward to your response. — Request interview

Sincerely yours,

Steven Foley
Steven Foley

▼ Practice

Find a want ad in the newspaper for a job opening that matches your qualifications. Pretend the want ad asks you to send a job application letter. Refer to your background information notes and fill out the job application form letter on page 135. Check the letter for errors, and write or type a final draft on your own paper. Note: If the ad does not give a name or position title to write to, begin your letter: *Dear Sir or Madam.*

_____
(your street address)

_____
(your city, state, and zip code)

_____
(date)

_____
(name of person, if stated in the ad)

_____
(company name)

_____
(street address)

_____
(city, state, and zip code)

Dear _____:
                       (person's name)

I would like to apply for the position of _____.
                                             (identify job title)

I meet the job requirements you described in _____.
                                          (identify source of the job ad)

_____
(summarize qualifications—work experience, skills, and so on)

_____

_____

_____

_____

_____

May I have an interview at your convenience? Please contact me at _____.
                                                       (your phone number)

I look forward to your response.

Sincerely,

_____
(signature)

_____
(printed name)

Job Application Forms

When you apply for jobs, you frequently will be asked to fill out job application forms. Your background information notes will help you provide accurate information about your experience and qualifications. In addition, you should use the following guidelines:

Guidelines for Filling Out Job Application Forms

- **Read the form first.** Identify the information you'll need to include.

- **Follow the instructions for filling out the form.** Carefully listen to any oral instructions and read the printed instructions.

- **Neatly print or type the information you provide.** Neat printing or typing is easier to read than cursive handwriting or sloppy printing.

- **Record the information in the appropriate places.** Be sure to write the information on the correct line or in the correct box.

- **Check your work for accuracy and completeness.** Double-check dates, names, and facts against your notes. Check your spelling. Make sure the form is complete.

▶ Jesse Santiago followed these guidelines as he filled out an application for a job as a delivery driver. Carefully read his two-page job application form on pages 137–138.

Application for Employment

Name ___Santiago_____Jesse_____P.___
             Last   First   Middle

Address ___5722 W. Melrose_____Chicago____IL.____60614___
             Street   City   State   Zip Code

Phone Number (312) 555-2168_____ Social Security Number 123-45-6789___
            Area Code

If you are not a U.S. citizen, can you legally work in the U.S.? ☒ Yes ☐ No

Are you 18 years old or older? ☒ Yes ☐ No

Position desired: ___Delivery driver_____

Date you can start: _____

Are you employed now? ☐ Yes ☒ No

If so, may we contact your employer? ☐ Yes ☐ No

Have you ever applied to this company before? ☐ Yes ☒ No

If so, when? _____

Employment Experience
(Start with your current or most recent job.)

Date (Month & Year)	Name and Address of Employer	Salary	Position	Reason for Leaving
From 11/89 To 5/91	Express Messenger Co. 315 S. Michigan Chicago, IL. 60614	$5.25/hour	Driver	layoffs
From 7/88 To 10/89	Mama's Pizza 1101 W. Armitage Chicago, IL. 60614	$4.50/hour	Delivery Driver	business closed
From To				

JOB APPLICANTS ARE REQUIRED TO ANSWER THE QUESTIONS BELOW ONLY IF THEY PERTAIN TO A BONA FIDE OCCUPATIONAL QUALIFICATION. **DO NOT ANSWER THESE QUESTIONS** IF EMPLOYER HAS NOT PLACED A CHECK ON THE LINE TO THE LEFT OF THE QUESTION.

_____ What is your height? _____

_____ What is your weight? _____

_____ What is your date of birth? _____

_____ Were you ever convicted of a felony or misdemeanor? If so, please describe:

_____

Education

	Name and Location	Did you graduate?	Describe course of study.
Grammar School	Taylor Elementary Chicago, IL.	Yes	General
High School	Dunbar High School Chicago, IL.	Yes	General
College			
Professional			

References

Name	Address	Profession	Years Acquainted
1 George Walsh	4105 W. Keystone Chicago, IL. 60697	Plumber	5
2 Rosa Flores	5531 S. Catalpa Chicago, IL. 60680	Restaurant Manager	4
3 Frank Liddell	6231 W. Paulina Chicago, IL. 60616	Car Mechanic	2

Statement

I certify that all information in this application is true and complete to the best of my knowledge. I authorize investigation of all statements contained herein. I understand that false or misleading information may result in my dismissal.

Jesse P. Santiago   _August 4, 199_
Signature of Applicant   Date

DO NOT WRITE BELOW THIS LINE

Hired? Yes   No

Position: _____

Interviewed by _____
Name and Position

Starting Date: _____

Salary/Hourly Rate: _____

_____
Date

▼ Practice

Select a job you feel you are qualified for and imagine you are applying for it. (You can get an idea from newspaper want ads.) Fill in the job application on the next two pages. Refer to your background information notes and follow the guidelines on page 136.

Application for Employment

Name _____

                Last   First   Middle

Address _____

           Street   City   State   Zip Code

Phone Number (_____) _____ Social Security Number _____

              Area Code

If you are not a U.S. citizen, can you legally work in the U.S.? ☐ Yes ☐ No

Are you 18 years old or older? ☐ Yes ☐ No

Position desired: _____

Date you can start: _____

Are you employed now? ☐ Yes ☐ No

If so, may we contact your employer? ☐ Yes ☐ No

Have you ever applied to this company before? ☐ Yes ☐ No

If so, when? _____

Employment Experience
(Start with your current or most recent job.)

Date (Month & Year)	Name and Address of Employer	Salary	Position	Reason for Leaving
From				
To				
From				
To				
From				
To				

Education

	Name and Location	Did you graduate?	Describe course of study.
Grammar School			
High School			
College			
Professional			

References

	Name	Address	Profession	Years Acquainted
1				
2				
3				

Statement

I certify that all information in this application is true and complete to the best of my knowledge. I authorize investigation of all statements contained herein. I understand that false or misleading information may result in my dismissal.

_____
Signature of Applicant   Date

DO NOT WRITE BELOW THIS LINE

Hired? Yes   No   Starting Date: _____

Position: _____   Salary/Hourly Rate: _____

Interviewed by _____   _____
                            Name and Position   Date

Preparing for an Interview

An **interview** is a formal conversation between an employer and a job applicant. During the interview, the employer, or interviewer, asks the job applicant a series of questions to determine whether or not the applicant is qualified for a job. Developing your skill in interviewing is important, since performing well at an interview can directly lead to a job offer.

What is your attitude toward job interviews? Do they make you feel nervous or anxious? These reactions are common because the outcome of the interview is important. However, you can overcome these feelings by preparing for the interview in advance.

- **Rehearse your answers to the interviewer's questions ahead of time.** On the next page are some questions frequently asked during job interviews. Practicing your responses in advance will help you communicate your qualifications more effectively during the actual interview.

- **Dress appropriately and neatly for the interview.** Plan what you are going to wear ahead of time. You'll feel more confident if you have paid attention to your personal appearance. You'll also make a favorable first impression on the interviewer. For an office job, men should wear a jacket and tie, and women should wear a suit or tailored outfit. See the pictures at the bottom of this page for examples.

- **Arrive 10 to 15 minutes early to the interview.** This will give you time to relax and think about what you want to tell the interviewer. You will also impress the interviewer with your punctuality.

Frequently Asked Interview Questions

Here is a list of frequently asked interview questions. In preparing for an interview, it can be helpful to rehearse the answers to these questions.

1. What jobs have you had? What were your responsibilities in these jobs?

2. Why did you leave these jobs?

3. What are your vocational or professional goals?

4. How much schooling do you have? What subjects did you like best?

5. How did you get along with your coworkers in previous jobs?

6. What do you know about our company?

7. Why do you want to work here? Why do you want this position?

8. Why do you think you're qualified for the job?

9. What kind of boss would you like to have?

10. Do you follow directions well?

11. Do you like working with others or by yourself?

12. What are your strengths and weaknesses at work?

13. Are you willing to work overtime? Are you willing to work evenings and weekends?

14. What was your salary on your last job? What salary do you want to earn here?

15. Can you provide references?

In addition, you should be prepared to answer questions specific to the job you are applying for. For example, if you are applying for a position as a receptionist, you may be asked how well you get along with the public. If you are applying for a data entry position, you may be asked how well you handle details.

▼ Practice

On a separate sheet of paper, briefly write the answers to three questions from the list above.

A Sample Interview

Marcia Swanson is interviewing Albert Gilmore for the position of counter assistant at Tastee Chicken, a fast-food restaurant. They are sitting in Marcia's office, located in the back of the restaurant. Two volunteers should read aloud the following dialogue.

Marcia: (*reading Albert's job application*) Albert, I see you've worked at Burger World for a year. What were your responsibilities?

Albert: I took orders, operated the cash register, and packaged the hamburgers and fries.

Marcia: I see. How did you get along with customers, especially during busy times?

Albert: I got along with customers fine. When it's busy, some customers get impatient, even angry. I just keep a cool head and try to work as fast as I can. I don't take angry customers' remarks personally.

Marcia: That's good to know. Some customers can be difficult, but we've got a rule around here—never argue with customers. Now to change the subject a little—our new employees go through a three-day training program here. Nothing real formal. If you're hired, you'll be assigned to work with an experienced counter assistant. He or she will show you the basics—operating our cash register, packaging the chicken, and so on. Would it bother you to take instructions from another coworker?

Albert: No problem. I'd just want to learn the job. When somebody explains how to do something, I try to follow their directions as best as I can.

Marcia: That's the kind of attitude we like our employees to have.

▼ Practice

1. Do you think Albert answered Marcia's questions effectively? Why or why not?

2. What is Marcia's impression of Albert? Give examples from the dialogue to support your answer.

3. Give an example of a question you were asked on an interview.

Nonverbal Communication:
Some Interview DO's and DON'Ts

DO greet your interviewer with a handshake.

DO maintain eye contact.

DON'T slouch in the chair. DON'T smoke or chew gum.

DON'T wear inappropriate clothes to an interview.

Writing a Resignation Letter

Most people don't remain with the same employer for their entire working lives. People change employers for various reasons—a better job offer, family obligations, and so on.

▶ Have you ever resigned from a job? If so, write your reason for quitting on the line below.

_____

You should carefully think through your decision to leave a job before you actually resign. Sometimes a frank discussion with your boss can help solve a problem. Also, it is to your advantage to find a new position before you resign.

If you do decide to resign from your job, you should tell your boss and then write a resignation letter. Generally, you should give your employer two weeks' notice of your intention to resign.

Your stated reason for leaving should sound positive, not negative. If you are resigning because of job dissatisfaction or personality conflicts, do *not* state this in the letter. Instead, you might say that you are resigning because you want to explore new job opportunities. A model resignation letter is shown below.

▼ Communication Tip

A resignation letter should include the following points:

- Date of resignation
- Announcement of resignation
- Positive reason for leaving
- Appreciation of the experience

Dear Ms. Falk:

Effective August 21, I will be resigning from my position at Polk Community Hospital. As I told you, I have decided to further my education. I have enrolled in the lab assistant program at Concord Junior College.

Thank you for your support during the past two years.

Sincerely,

Norma Ortiz

Norma Ortiz

▼ Practice

Think of a job you have resigned from. (Or if you have not resigned from a job, imagine that you have.) Write a resignation letter on a separate sheet of paper.

WORKING TOGETHER

Directions: This activity will help you practice your interviewing skills. Choose a partner to work with. Each of you will take turns playing the roles of an interviewer and a job applicant. Guidelines for both of these roles follow. Afterward, you will meet with your partner to discuss each other's interview.

INTERVIEWER'S GUIDELINES

1. Carefully read your partner's filled-out job application on pages 139–140. Familiarize yourself with his or her background and work experience.

2. Based on the job position your partner wants, write a list of questions to ask. You may also choose some questions from the list on page 142.

3. Greet your partner and introduce yourself.

4. Sit in chairs facing each other. Maintain eye contact with your partner throughout the interview.

5. Begin asking your partner the interview questions.

6. Listen carefully to your partner's responses. If an answer is too brief, ask for additional details.

7. Invite your partner to ask questions about the job. Be creative in your answers.

8. After 10 to 15 minutes, conclude the interview. Tell your partner when you will make your hiring decision.

JOB APPLICANT'S GUIDELINES

1. Show your partner your filled-out job application.

2. Greet your partner and introduce yourself.

3. Listen carefully to your partner's questions. Answer clearly and concisely. Do not get sidetracked or give unnecessary details.

4. Do not make negative statements about previous jobs or supervisors.

5. Maintain eye contact with your partner throughout the interview. Lean forward slightly in your chair.

6. Control signs of nervousness—for example, avoid clenching your fists, tapping your foot, and so on. Try to keep a pleasant, interested expression on your face.

7. At the end of the interview, thank your partner for interviewing you.

For Discussion: After the interview, discuss this question with each other:
Based on the interview, would you hire your partner for the job? Give reasons to explain your answer.

Is Honesty the Best Policy?

Larry Costello is interviewing for the position of stock clerk at a supermarket. In the script below, Peter Huston, the interviewer, is asking questions about Larry's former job.

Peter: Larry, could you tell me why you left your job at Randall's Supermarket?

Larry: Sure. My boss didn't know how to supervise people. I know he had it in for me from the start. He just didn't like me. He criticized everything I did. After a while, I just got fed up, so I quit.

Peter: You know, that situation with your former boss concerns me. Do you have a problem getting along with supervisors?

Larry: No problem, as long as they treat me fairly. My boss didn't like some of my coworkers, either. They disliked him, too, because he was always giving orders. As I said, he just didn't know how to supervise people.

Peter: How did you get along with your coworkers?

Larry: Great, except for this one cashier. She really got on my nerves. She was always asking me to do price checks for her. Usually, it was a waste of my time. The price would be taped on the food, but for some reason, she didn't see it. Of course, my boss never criticized her because he liked her.

Peter: Well, Larry, at our store teamwork is important. I expect everyone to cooperate with one another. I have the impression that you have problems cooperating with other employees.

Larry: No, that's not true. I know how to cooperate with other people, but it works two ways. Other employees have to cooperate with me, too. I do my job as best as I can, and they have to realize my time is important. Like that cashier I was telling you about—I cooperated with her, but she wasn't cooperating with me.

▼ For Discussion

1. During an interview, should a job applicant criticize a former boss? Give reasons to explain your answer.

2. If you were Peter, would you hire Larry? Give reasons to explain your answer.

3. How do you define cooperation? Why is cooperation among employees important?

Communication Skills Review

Part A

Directions: Read the dialogue below and answer the questions about both workers.

Paul Hassan is a clerical assistant at Cormax Machine Company. Several other clerical assistants work in the office with him. Paul frequently types letters and memos on a computer. One day, the computer stops functioning correctly. Paul looks through the computer handbook, but he can't solve the problem, so he calls the computer assistance service.

Elva: Elva Spears, Computers Unlimited. May I help you?

Paul: Hello. This is Paul Hassan from Cormax Machine Company. Our computer isn't working. I thought you could help us find the problem.

Elva: Certainly. What are the make and serial number?

Paul: Just a minute. I'll go check. (*two minutes later*) It's a PST Quickwriter, and the number is AM 4270895.

Elva: (*taking notes*) A PST Quickwriter, AM 4270896.

Paul: No—the last four digits are oh eight nine *five*.
Elva: Got it. And which word processing system do you use?

Paul: WordOrder 7.0.

Elva: All right, what exactly is the problem?

Paul: It's stuck. Every time I hit a key, the computer makes a beeping noise. Then a sentence appears on the screen that says *Error: invalid command*.

Elva: Do you remember what you were doing right before you got stuck?

Paul: No. I'd have to think about it for a minute. Could I call you back?

Elva: That would be fine. Talk to you later.

Paul made the call.
1. Did Paul introduce himself adequately?

2. Was he polite?

3. Was Paul prepared for the call? Give examples to support your view.

4. Imagine that you are making the call to Elva. What information should you have together before you call? Write it below in the form of notes.

```
                        Notes




```

Elva received the call.

5. Did Elva identify herself adequately?

6. Was she polite and helpful to Paul? Give examples to support your answer.

7. Were Elva's questions effective? Why or why not?

Part B

Directions: Read the information below and then write Paul's memo.

On the second phone call to Elva, Paul found out that he had made a mistake. When he had gotten stuck on the computer, he had randomly pressed different keys. Elva told him that he should stop and get help when he gets stuck. She told him that randomly pressing keys could cause him to lose his work.

Paul told his supervisor about his conversation with Elva. His supervisor said that many of the other clerical assistants had been getting stuck on the computer too. She asked Paul to write a memo summarizing what he had learned from Elva.

Write Paul's memo using the format below. Include

- a description of the computer problem and the proposed solution

- the name and phone number of the computer assistance service and the first and last name of Paul's contact there.

Memorandum

To: _____   Subject: _____

From: _____   Date: _____

_____

_____

_____

_____

_____

_____

_____

_____

Answer Key

Lesson 1
Page 4: Practice
Answers will vary.

Page 5: Practice
Answers will vary.

Page 8: Practice

Lesson 2
Answers will vary.

Page 12: Practice
Answers will vary.

Page 13: Practice
Answers will vary.

Page 15: Practice
Part A
1. "What does *ream* mean?"
2. The office clerk wasted time and will have to make another trip to the supply room.

Part B
Answers will vary.

Page 16: Practice
Answers will vary.

Lesson 3
Page 20: Practice
Part A
1. Asking or urging a person to do something
2. Exchanging opinions or feelings
3. Commenting immediately about something you see, hear, touch, taste, or smell (OR Reporting or getting information)
4. Reporting or getting information
5. Solving a problem

Part B
Answers will vary.

Page 23: Practice
1. The topic is a description of a hit-and-run accident.
2. The police officer is the audience.
3. Yes—the speaker says, "I've gone over everything I saw in my mind."
4. The message is a sequence of events listed in time order.
5. The eyewitness offers to answer other questions.

Lesson 4
Page 29: Practice
Part A
Answers may vary. Here are some possible answers:
1. "I'm surprised!" *raised eyebrows, opened mouth*
2. "I'm angry." *cold stare, no eye contact, frown*
3. "I'm busy." *looking at watch, preoccupied with another activity, avoiding eye contact*

Part B
Answers will vary.

Page 30: Practice
Answers will vary. Here are some possible answers.
1. Janine slouched, put her foot on an empty chair, examined her fingernails, looked at her watch, raised her eyebrows, and sighed.
2. The director may have thought Janine was bored or that she didn't like the director's idea.
3. No. Janine was excited about the plan and eager to get to work.
4. She could have sat up straight in her chair and looked alert and interested.

Lesson 5
Page 34: Practice
Part B
Answers will vary. Here is a sample of what your paper would look like if you followed the directions.

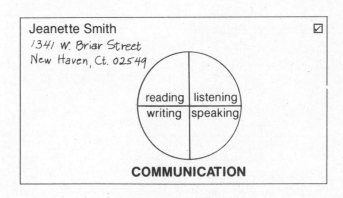

Page 36: Practice
The correct order is 4, 2, 5, 1, 3.

Page 37: Practice
1. Sorting the morning mail is the topic
2. Answers may vary. A suggested answer is shown below.
   1. sort mail according to departments
   2. pull envelopes marked *special delivery* and *certified mail*
   3. sort envelopes into these two categories
   4. wrap rubber band around each type of letter
   5. put banded envelopes on top of right department stack

Page 38: Practice
Wording of notes may vary. Here is a suggested list of steps:
1. insert card into slot
2. hold in place for a moment
3. wait for light and buzzer
4. push down door handle
5. remove card

Lesson 6
Page 42: Practice
Answers will vary.

Page 43: Practice
Questions will vary. Examples of questions are shown below.
A. How long have you been a babysitter? Who else have you worked for? What is your hourly rate? When would you be able to start? Why did you decide to become a babysitter?
B. How much is the rent? When is the rent due? Who pays for the heat and water? Is the apartment close to public transportation and shopping? What is the neighborhood like?

Page 44: Practice
Answers should include the following information:
1. Prepare questions in advance and write them down.
2. Postpone asking questions when the boss is busy.
3. Ask her boss to arrange a time for answering her questions.

Lesson 7
Pag 48: Practice
Answers will vary.

Page 51: Practice
Answers will vary. Here are some sample answers:
1. Walter finds out that Audrey has never used a time clock before. Therefore, he gives more background information and details. He also uses language she understands.
2. His illustrations are clear, accurate, friendly, well organized, and complete. For example, he describes each step of the punching process. He asks to make sure Audrey has understood.
3. The person can directly observe someone else performing the task. It's easier to form and keep a mental picture that way.
4. Audrey restates Walter's explanation in her own words.

Page 52: Practice
Answers will vary.

Lesson 8
Page 56: Practice
1. Nancy says "Hello" to both callers. However, she is much more informal when ending the conversation with her friend than when saying good-bye to the service representative.
2. Nancy uses casual words like *same old thing*, *yeah*, and *see ya*.
3. No. She is much more formal during the business call.

Page 58: Practice
Answers will vary. Here are some possible answers:
1. No. Words in the script used to describe Ms. Smith's tone of voice reveal her rudeness. For example, "speaking fast," "interrupting," and "sighing loudly" show her inconsiderate attitude.
2. No. Ms. Smith misspells Ms. Gámez's name, even though Ms. Gámez gave her the correct spelling over the phone. Ms. Smith is also impatient with Ms. Gámez's questions.
3. Ms. Smith uses the abbreviation *CBC* and the technical term *complete blood count*, which Ms. Gámez does not understand.

Page 59: Practice
Answers will vary. Here are some possible answers:
1. Yes. For example, Ms. Smith uses courteous expressions, such as "I'll be happy to check," "please," and "you're welcome."
2. Yes. When Ms. Smith answers the phone, she states her name and the name of her workplace.
3. Ms. Smith provides as much information as she can, so Ms. Gámez asks only a few questions.

Lesson 9
Page 66: Practice
Answers will vary. Here are some possible answers:
1. Jake, the caller, is responsible. He did not properly identify himself, and the information he gave Anna was incomplete. Furthermore, Jake acted annoyed when Anna was unable to help him.
2. No. Jake was unprepared to give Anna the facts that she needed, such as the account and purchase order numbers.
3. No. To cancel the order, Anna did not need to know about the inventory clerk's mistake. Even if she did need to know the reason for the cancellation, it was unprofessional of Jake to openly criticize a coworker.

Page 67: Practice
Answers will vary. Here are some possible answers:
1. Yes. Jake responded to Anna's questions quickly and concisely. He provided accurate information because he obviously had a copy of the purchase order handy.
2. He was helpful, polite, businesslike, appreciative, and respectful.
3. Yes. As an employee, Jake represented his company, R&W Insurance. Since Jake was organized and businesslike, Anna probably has a favorable impression of his company.

Page 68: Practice
Answers will vary.

Lesson 10
Page 73: Practice
Answers will vary.

Page 76: Practice
The following statements should have a check mark: 3, 5, 8, 10.

Lesson 11
Page 80: Practice
Answers will vary.

Page 81: Practice
Answers will vary.

Page 82: Practice
Answers will vary.

Lesson 12
Page 90: Practice
Answers will vary. Check to see that you printed in pen and filled out the entire form.

Lesson 13
Page 91: Practice
Answers will vary slightly. Your message form should look similar to the one below.

IMPORTANT MESSAGE

FOR Maggie Donaldson

DATE 4/9   TIME 3:15 A.M. (P.M.)

MS. Jody Stein

OF Hi-Tech Software

PHONE 555-7111 x 914
AREA CODE   NUMBER   EXTENSION

TELEPHONED	✓	PLEASE CALL	
CAME TO SEE YOU		WILL CALL AGAIN	
RETURNED YOUR CALL		**URGENT**	

MESSAGE Wants to schedule sales meeting

SIGNED Dale Nowinski

Page 92: Practice
Answers will vary. A sample form is shown below.

C&R CORPORATION COPY REQUISITION

Number of copies of each original needed 50

Number of originals (each side is an original) 10

☒ One-sided   ☒ Collated

☐ Two-sided   ☐ Collated and stapled

Copies are usually to be run on white paper. If you want colored paper, please specify color.

Brief description of originals (title, opening words, etc.)
C + R Training Programs

Special instructions Punch holes for a 3-ring binder

Copies needed by (date) 10/14   Time Current Time

Requested by Your name   Date of request 10/11
(print your name)

Lesson 13
Page 97: Practice
Answers will vary. Make sure that all of the activities from page 96 appear on your schedule.

Page 98: Practice
Part A
Answers will vary. Below is a sample list of things to do.

| Invite friends | Buy food and decorations |
| Plan menu | Clean house |

Part B
Answers will vary.

Page 99: Practice

Answers will vary. Here are some possible answers.

1. A supervisor can help an employee decide which tasks are most important.
2. She might not have completed all of the tasks. If the tasks weren't written down, she might have forgotten one of them.

Page 100: Practice

Answers will vary. Possible answers are shown below.

1. He seems disorganized.
2. His work habits might be sloppy.
3. Yes. He probably has trouble finding things he needs.

Lesson 14

Page 104: Practice

Answers will vary.

Page 105: Practice

Answers will vary.

Page 106: Practice

1. b
2. a
3. d

Page 107: Practice

Your memo should be similar to the following:

TO: All Employees   **DATE:** August 3, 199—

FROM: (Your Name)   **SUBJECT:** New Schedule for Mail Pickups

The mail room has changed its schedule for picking up outgoing mail. The new schedule will go into effect on August 10. The mail room clerk will pick up the mail twice in the morning and twice in the afternoon.

Morning Pickups	Afternoon Pickups
9:30 A.M.	1:30 P.M.
11 A.M.	4:30 P.M.

Page 108: Practice

Answers will vary.

Lesson 15

Page 113: Practice

Part A

1. c
2. f
3. e
4. a
5. b
6. d

Part B

Answers will vary.

Page 115: Practice

1. 432 North Moss Road
   New Orleans, LA 70119
   September 6, 199—
2. Mr. Jim Lowell
   Lowell's Muffler Shop
   6034 North Clark Street
   Louisville, KY 40201
3. Dear Mr. Lowell:
4. Truly yours,
5. 120 West Fulton Avenue
   Dallas, TX 75080
   November 3, 199—
6. Ms. Carol Andrews
   1400 West Bucaro Avenue
   Dallas, TX 75080
7. Dear Ms. Andrews:
8. Congratulations! You have just won a free trip to Jamaica.
9. Sincerely yours,

Lesson 16

Page 122: Practice

Answers will vary.

Page 123: Practice

1. Answers will vary.
2. Answers will vary.
3. The words *insurance, canceled,* and *Kenmore* are misspelled. The first letter of each word in *Safeway Auto Insurance Company* should be capitalized. The abbreviation *Ave.* should be spelled out as *Avenue.*

Page 126: Practice

Answers will vary.

Lesson 17

Page 132: Practice

Answers will vary.

Page 134: Practice

Answers will vary. Make sure you have checked your letter for errors.

Page 142: Practice

Answers will vary.

Page 143: Pratice

Answers will vary. Possible answers are shown below.

1. Yes. He described his duties clearly and displayed a cooperative attitude.
2. She has a good impression of him. At the end of the dialogue she says, "That's the kind of attitude we like our employees to have."
3. Answers will vary.

Page 145: Practice

Answers will vary.

COMMUNICATION SKILLS REVIEW:
Pages 148–150

Part A

Answers may vary but should be similar to the following:

1. Yes. Paul introduces himself with his name and the name of his company.
2. No. He is rather impolite: he makes Elva wait for two minutes while he checks on the make and serial number.
3. No. He is unprepared for the call: he does not have the make and serial number of the computer, and he has not thought about the problem carefully.
4.

> -Call Computers Unlimited-555-3657
> -PST Quickwriter-#AM 4270895
> -Word Order 7.0
> -Computer is stuck, beeps
> -Screen says Error: invalid command
> -I was typing a memo and must have hit the wrong Key.

5. Yes. When Elva answers the phone, she says her full name and the name of the company.
6. Yes. She uses polite language ("May I help you," "Certainly," "That would be fine." Also, she patiently waits for Paul to return with the information she needs.
7. Yes. Elva asked specific questions to get the information she needed.

Part B

Answers may vary. Here is a possible response:

> ### Memorandum
>
> To: All computer users Subject: Recent computer problems
> From: Paul Hassan   Date: April 28, 199~
>
> Recently, many of us have had difficulties using the computers. We have been informed that we should stop immediately when we get stuck and seek help. For advice on solving computer problems, call Elva Spears at Computers Unlimited. The phone number is 555-3657.
> To save time, make sure you have all the necessary information about your problem before you make the call.